EARLY LINOLEUM

EARLY LINOLEUM

BRENDA IIJIMA

Counterpath   Denver   2015

Counterpath
Denver, Colorado
www.counterpathpress.org

Library of Congress Cataloging-in-Publication Data
Iijima, Brenda.
 [Prose works. Selections]
 Early linoleum / Brenda Iijima.
   pages cm
 ISBN 978-1-933996-42-4 (softcover : acid-free paper)
I. Title.
 PS3559.I35A6 2014
 818'.54—dc23
                    2014034835

EARLY LINOLEUM

A *Caliban and the Witch* refrain. I'm compelled to quote from Silvia Federici's *Caliban and the Witch* repeatedly as a form of rehabilitating dubious historical accounts that have been buried subcutaneously—to rally around rebellious claims for the gendered, administered bodies that we are, and the textual artifice where we arrange edifices of our embodied experiences. The woodcuts of the world begin to vocalize their subversive, utopian dimensions, blaspheme is whispered in the wind and a somatic commotion stimulates politics animistically. Important rocks, significant rocks. Never to be used again to stone women. Never again to be carved into pompous heroic figures. She was chained naked to a rock on the coast of Annisquam; a flock of seabirds gave her methods to free herself. The seabirds might have been her imaginative brainwaves: a hallucination of presence radiating outside her body. Dynamic primal space always couples with the social, otherwise she wouldn't find herself restrained by this problem. Squam rock is an immense boulder located on a hill in a residential part of Annisquam (part of Gloucester proper), Massachusetts. An epic mound of compression linked and locked to the land, a continent clamored over by numerous human-animals in their youth. A bulky molecular entity surrounded by a visceral and glandular world. Everything is straw/is rock. (Etel Adnan) Kate, did you happen upon the *YouTube* video that a son recorded of his mother attempting to climb up Squam Rock? In your childhood, this was a rite of passage, a social requirement: to scale the precarious granite spine of the rock and find momentary social acceptance. There's no way to get a proper running start necessary to generate the momentum it takes to scale it, there's a precipice that could send you plunging down. The rock is an entity of magnitude and gravity. It compels identification and response.

There was a tiny princess stuck down with the booze until the toads suck days, it's a city thing—there are rides and popcorn, kids have races—one event that is on-going is stuck on a truck. The visiting professor interrupted a private narrative and superimposed a declarative presumption upon the setting that predisposed a wavering condition. There was cultural pressure to talk about ourselves as gendered beings. This was a man speaking. The conflicts produced confused flows of contradictory information in the early days of the crisis. The citizens suspended their hopes and beliefs. As the days passed time flowed messily, any semblance of chronology disappeared. Outbreak of violence and fear plus a spectrum of subtle unnamable emotions arose and dissipated between persons. Communally and individually the responsive fabric shivered. One could peer out momentarily at the similarity of thinking as the texture of experience transitioned into densely interwoven differentiation with certain improbabilities presented over and again as a compulsive neurological pattern was coming to the surface. Physical mixtures synthesize at extreme temperatures. Bodies from other geological eras provide our energy; these bodies when burned give off poisonous gasses, accelerating the effect of burning, which cycles the planet toward prodigious change. There is an urgent need to protect all the transformers on the grid from surges caused by geomagnetic disturbances such as electro-static sparks. Weather patterns follow this scenario of emergency management. Solar energy is attracted to the rock. She gripped the rock personally-impersonally.

As a set of conditions become an immersive subject the essence of production vanishes. Money seems to contain human subjectivity. Water seems to also. Electric traces create a maze—impulses confirm surface tensions, submerged significance coiled and combining. The proliferation of searchable public images in a corporate-military cloud burgeons—crucial when thinking about presence. There's nothing to focus on that resembles subject *working on the self* when problematized by mechanized enslavement. What is being discussed here is expanse, often referred to as a totalizing gaze. Mass produced as bodies of feeling. The focus was on the means of our conditioning and how to navigate these terms through somatic response. That stump was energetic, mentality stung by electric surges as barriers dissolved between objects. Our electric unified global brain signals depth charges in the now. Dio has an auxiliary brain that you invented and also destroyed. She's a fictionalized character from the fibers of your neurological wiring—evidence that you've downloaded your brain. Robert Smithson tried to demonstrate how entropy functions within an aesthetic modality. He used geological elements to elaborate how perception is shifted as energy in the universe dissipates; there is increased randomness and disorder eventuating social upheaval and eventually heat death. Minerals in our body react to gravity and this has an effect on behavior, culturally and otherwise. There are biometric profiles stored in government databanks. Movement is tracked. Drones focus in on readymade, supplied targets. Killing machines in theaters of war and or civic space when the state feels it needs to eliminate someone. *YouTube* videos of the warzones are filled with the relentless sound of their whirring. Space is in flux, gyrating possibility like in the case of the choreographed piece I danced as cars drove by through the force field of performance. Balancing on the stump. Visceral archives coagulate the on-going condition of being. Every attempt made to circumvent the militarization of intelligence. Deterritorialization acts on our social needs and desires by distributing affective histories across a web. The dissipation of energy is an on-going event, everything requires recharging. Immensity, scale, observation. Wake up feeling devastated, not being able to apprehend the season. The apes viewed the plinth with curiosity and suspicion for good reason—remember that scene? We pick it, hunt it, gather it and catalogue it: telemetry and telescope tracking, chips and ankle bracelets. And so I was saying, I found myself sitting on a huge boulder in the forest talking to you about the color green, (also apperception) thoughts came as a fluid transmission. The boulder, one could feel this, had been puked up from inner earth and had crumbled, after which it had been pushed down the mountain by the collecting force of an ice age. Before that an ocean sat upon it. Blizzards of various weapons swirled about me. In this manner they strove to obstruct my meditation. But with my intuitive understanding fully charged, my awareness expanded, my insight's nerves opened, attaining irreversible faith, I sang. (Lady Yeshe Tsogyal) You and I, we sit together analyzing rebellion as a social form. We discuss aspects of insurrections, revolts and riots. We know the authorities are doing the same: dictating strategies about crowd control, bodies acting out civil disobedience and rebelling. When there is an overload an irreconcilable barrier presents a situation with impasse. Now we are guerrilla fighters in preparation. Half the time we are joking. The whole continent is a danger zone in a sense—the police state extends its rule universally. They have commands and ultimatums like, if the unit is ambushed, the most important counteraction is for all available personnel to return fire as rapidly as possible. They see everything in four dimensions (maximum outsized technologies). All we want to do is get from the site point to the row of mirrors shoring up the earth at degree zero. You are hesitant to swim long distances so how do you expect us to transition the lake? Toshi is of course already on the other side, amused by our dilemma. Will we have time to build a raft and what material can we salvage in this desert! The most closely related passage in his published "the Spiral Jetty" essay (1972) is somewhat less sanguinary but more carnal in its circling back toward his youthful conjuring of "the chopped meat of paradise:" (Thomas Crow) "Surely, the storm clouds massing would turn into a rain of blood. Once, when I was flying over the lake, its surface seemed to hold all the properties of an unbroken field of raw meat with gristle (foam); no doubt it was due to some freak wind action. Eyesight is often slaughtered by the other senses, and when that happens it becomes necessary to seek out dispassionate abstractions. (Robert Smithson) Radiant energy follows along the meridian of a childhood reverie at the memorial for veterans on the mountain circa 1978 and streams to centers in the brain in your current body where it becomes intrinsic. The negative charge is electricity. You will contend with this dream your whole life. You will relate its narrative in living form. You are compelled to; it is electrically charged. Electricity seeks out positive charge. It is a focal point in the land of awareness and a metaphor for body practice. Today, tomorrow: infinity. A dream is a phenomenon of the whispering of the brain. I sat on the boulder in the forest by the stream as a technique to enhance this contemplative meme. The scenes that followed convinced her that she had not yet fathomed the obscure gulph into which she had plunged. (Mary Shelly) A culture buried in snow. Skip a rock into prelingual reality. It's great to keep my empire in a computer made of hearts I keep in my machine. (Anne Boyer) Most things are being made in the imperial style (resource acquisition)—its part of the industrial blueprint. The crowd, yourself, furniture. (Lauren Levin) You heard some news and knelt. You heard some news and laughed. You heard some news and your skin cracked. You heard some news and your chest crashed. (R. Erica Doyle)

Seriously,
lime pit where employees hack away at rocks
—shareholders *own* the mountain—reps
get all pink and huffy telling us so
We wonder, is it private property to the molten core?
Around their epic factory pock marked pits of the hill
Glowing blue ponds of off-flow quarantined to reach inertia
Entropic—burn of ankles should we linger longer
The universe contrasts these functions
Hack off a portion of the mountain
Crush it down for our staples, like toothpaste pharmaceutical
The mountain, a broken tooth
Shall we access the back terrain surreptitiously?
You worry about setting off the dynamite
Dance is performed on the ledge as an afterworld to presence
Thanks for being the sole onlooker
Rhythmic dancer enveloped, stitched, to perform scenes
in harsh daylight, disappear into body fragments

Soiled blanket found in the woods behind the house
Pearled muddy crocheted mustard yellow moldy ripped
Choreography, dirt, ungulate sunset, drape around torso
Dog pound below yelping here crime scene, missing bodies
Twisting arms, contorted mutating disabled distended beauty
Dancing a continuum of land
Tears in the eyes and a thick feeling in the throat
Collecting footage for a film about sludge
Administering our futures with primal eyes
Heartening to compare notes on our toxic-laden
childhoods—we say we have the syndrome
A tip of hat to the old shoe factory and worker's disputes
Once booming factory town left as an archeological remain but
there's a city hall and a mayor, 4 supermarkets and at least 6 churches plus
        a synagogue. This valley town with high hills encircling...

The move from the lingual to the shadow-perceptual non-voice anticipates and prompts cognitive changes in the body: thinking is altered, body chemically adjusts. That dirty blanket that I came upon in the forest— forlorn, abandoned—evocative discarded intimate handmade intricacy. Found wrapped around rotting leaves. Squelched realizations in wooded areas decoy hegemonic considerations. Rancid leaves and growth didn't decay the blanket; it is made of polyester, hand crocheted. Death lingers around it, murmurs under it. There is a rampant history held over these woods. Common dress, body un-partitioned. Fucking/forest/ fucking in said forest (we did). This blanket is stained above a nude quotidian. Right now it's at my parent's house, spread on the sofa. At the time unemployed men smoked and drank in the woods, the lush zone behind my childhood home. They'd be hunched over and passed out or hunched over talking or not talking, sometimes burning stuff. I often aimed my handsome handmade bow and arrow at them, whoever *the they* was on a particular day. How mean can you get with murder? Sequences where murder is the taste of tongues. Seriously, and waterways. Silty mounds channel the surging liquid. On these islands, quartz to suggest the massive compression of worlds. Look through water to see monster magnitude. The water was infused with a way of life. (Laura Moriarty) Nude limbs. Running through the forest naked is animal if you do so undetectably from those that refer to themselves as human. To watch them from behind a bush doing their human things, sometimes pissing or jacking off which at least meant they were preoccupied. Women! Stay out of the woods—this unspoken warning (Hélène Cixous). I'd pay tribute to the broadcasted fear by marching right up to the ancient white pine tree and displaying myself to the old growth. Last summer, movement research in the form of wolf dances conceived on the decomposing stump. I thought of this as getting real. Corporeal consequences engendered by finding the blanket. Ugly and menacing, a trial to escape social subjugation. The trees breathe so gorgeously. The river breathes. Stones covered with slippery algae are alive, dancing these realities. Later you can imagine there are no women taking a line from Joan Copjec. In the understory of meaning the locus shifts to sublimation's adversary, the cruelly uncreative superego, as Copjec analyzes Kant's unwieldy concept of radical evil, envy's corruption of liberal demands for equality and justice, and the difference between sublimation and perversion. The all-seeing underbrush conveys absorption, not hysteria. Hysteria is quickly blotted out (screams are muted) the hyperreal is not silent; it buzzes at the micro level of sound. These are the screams of terror on TV we've absorbed. Continual attempts to search for the trace residuals of her body, their bodies. The magnitude of instantiation (death) is a surrounding factor, like the atmosphere. Initially the boundary of death seriously offends, but death is not an opposing world breaking up the visible. Reassurance and ecstasy follow the realization. The tensions of empire in my childhood were about disappearance and retention loss, trace decay and interferences, without getting into the methodological considerations and slights of hand because many begged to differ and *remembered*. When I dug around for her torso I searched for her memory. I lay awkwardly in the pit crudely dug for her supine body (hacked). The blanket was the shroud. Remorselessly apparent silence. Someone had created this form of mustard colored yarns—gendered female, the form of the blanket. The sound of the ding-dong cart created cognitive dissonance when within forest's cover. For 45 cents, a Bomb Pop®, my sister gorged herself on icy rockets! An hour before the sugar ritual the emergency sirens would blare. My mom mowed the challenging slope. Butch mother, femme father. A tender moment: my father gracefully combing his hair. Grease your knees in the realm of this maniacal undertow where lawns buckle and front doors vomit the effluvium of industry in the form of bleach, chloride, methane and other noxious chemical vapors. We must be the disposable population or is that just about everyone by now. It is no longer necessary to think in the strict sense of inclusion-exclusion; one falls off the conveyor belt at any juncture. When we folded the mechanics rags she whispered steal a few, go ahead. I couldn't look at you because we were each in our own cubicle and the conveyor belt wouldn't stop. Minimum wage was classified as fast food. Body experiences interstitially between play, labor, torture and sleep. New project development in the former brickyard. A mini village of townhouses the planners called a project with skylights; modern accoutrements. Made of fiberboard and glued product, new materials drenched in formaldehyde. Kids sometimes refuse to walk and thus roll their way to destinations on an open grid. We rarely spoke English. On hindsight the recognition of social planning and economic resource comes into focus; the shifts of affect in the brick and mortar to find out where one is. Cambodia was being carpet bombed as we rolled around in the sun. Proximity hallucinations with war forever atmospheric condition. Shadows of bullet sprays and white phosphorescence, Noxzema™ ghost facing pre-grave twitter, posthumous affects as executive orders. We didn't cooperate, we didn't give anything, and we didn't give over or give in. Shook up and shook out—iterations of shaken known as expropriation. That's why we spent so much time recollecting at the dump. MacArthur Park is melting in the dark. All the sweet, green icing flowing down. Someone left the cake out in the rain. I don't think that I can take it 'cause it took so long to bake it and I'll never have that recipe again, oh no. Donna Summer, always. The school report delivered on the My Lai massacre, dented. Indented. Body pock marks and deep grooves of visceral depths, tis a swamp and a functioning ventricle system pushing blood to brain centers. This vow not to reproduce in the face of militarized body expectations: conflating an historical event with the body which didn't directly participate, body implicated belatedly. Our wars are affective tissue. Here's a proposal to misguide the body. Place these terms on the body—they were placed there—internalized, carved with fate lines. Motives to skin the shadow within the mainframe of mechanized social fabric. Reasons fail-reasons to fail. The necessity for a steady stream of soldiers and cogs in the machine—reproductive necessities. All the shit jobs, *undistributing the catch*. Stagflation overgrowth, a deciduous social platform teeters. Special thanks to that distraction is the most cynical utterance "it" can make. Stint at Kmart. There was blue light for the massive inventory scarcity curated around themes of domesticity and beautification. Delve into crosscurrents when passing isles of merchandise at once alienated from source and sense but not sensation. At the time, stocking bedware, traveling into your world, you who will sleep on plump polyester forms, me and another teen named Dawn. Torn away weight numbers. Body conditioning. Supreme. Palimpsest ghost. The living trace in the vicinity of spent fuel ponds. The working body is immersive, disappears. Welcome mat of glass shards, a toast in the house of regenerative cells. We will not be excused. What presents itself is a chain of integral events. Blanket living presence of forest pain—wyrdness, the haunting blanket / this hyper essay riven with memory so I looked up wyrd and it happens that wyrd is a feminine noun, and its Norse cognate urðr, besides meaning 'fate', is the name of one of the Norns (female beings who rule the destiny of gods and men); urðr is literally 'that which has come to pass, verðandi is what is in the process of happening' (the present participle of the verb cognate to weorþan) and skuld 'debt, guilt' (from a Germanic root skul- 'to owe', also found in English shall). An active boundary with death—as Leslie explicates: time's active past, present and future operates at this border. Especially active at the site of difference. Pain is magnified in this imperial nightmare.

Sand, shells, oil. Burning timber. The house across the street had been relocated from the mountaintop during the 19th century. When the Millers purchased the house from the Hawthorne family they found out that the basement was filled with marijuana, stealthily concealed—a former tenant, before going to jail, had stashed his grass in the root cellar. Mushrooms grew on the window sills. The house was fabricated from the wood of the mountain, hand hewn oak and maple. My nemesis lived there for a time. The Lacanian big Other. Her rusty nails and her misshapen bite—machinations. She'd crouch by the low hedges beside our small white ranch house, contemplating her next move. We never locked our doors. How glad I was that time eliminated the threat of her physical presence. Stuff of the Manson family; big Other was meant to be with their kin. Although, perhaps she was more like Jeffrey Dahmer because big Other was seemingly a loner (when not stalking prey). Rendition in an eco chamber, the gloved hand of Mars. When you want to come you have to first go, as in shut the door which is a human gateway: we all must succumb to the door, or live out-of-doors. She wears a poncho I had thought would only look attractive on someone taller. She stands solemnly at the subway platform, beyond the yellow rubberized safety line, rats on the tracks, cacophonous noises jar the senses. From this angle I can see one shoulder and what would be her hip, the poncho completely cloaks her physical form. The thickly painted support column is muted green off-glow, hulky, forked in the underground. I'm making my way to an intimate memorial gathering to honor Akilah Oliver at Anne Waldman's place. The day is windy and bloodless. The train interior smells of alcohol evaporating through the pores of the passengers. There is a blank spot in time caused by transition—a colorless, odorless blank. The tenderness of the gathering and the realization of a vernacular archive begin to fill the blank, instantiating meaning once again. Our bodies have a difficult time holding so many meanings simultaneously as the death toll rises. The profane reality of death floats over surfaces while also saturating deeply within the cells. I found this to be true when I collected the oral histories of residents of the town as they remembered the murders of young women in that town that took place in the 1970's and 1980's. This confirms the meanings lodged in the body, as blood pulses through meaning. Her body was dissected in the hotel room and then disposed of through the laundry chute. A search party began looking in the forest. This is not to dwell morosely on past 'events' as if contained in thought bubbles privately and inexplicably floating above skulls. Leakage throughout the corpus. We could go there now and resist uncovering what we intended to locate.

GLOSSEMATICS, THUS

That independence is the very principle of glossematics as the formal science of language.

JACQUES DERRIDA, *Of Grammatology*

Monkey struts up to the elephant with a lie about the lion.

TYRONE WILLIAMS, *AAB*

Ummm,   , ~~killer~~ killeth
     Or
Fixated attention on <u>or</u>

A hinge articulates the entire argument: the full daylight of presence avoids the dangerous supplement.

My life or your life——other other m/other
Pulsating ventricles surge the membrane/your brain/my brain: hello

                                        Hello
There

Or is where?

Desire or need; the home of two origins, southern or northern, is already assured.

The owl flies in the moonlight, over a field where the wounded cry out
Wounds bring all the colors into proximity

Flying over the dirt and trees the super ego flies
Since this tree was eaten it is now a squirrel
Can't go there
Boundary: gravity, the invisible line, leg mechanisms won't take me
Heavy like this morsel
There are steel bars occluding a vision
What is done in the now, now
A site where nothing is elicited

This thought has no weight. It is, in the play of the system, that very thing which never has weight.

When born— weighed 6 pounds— wriggled in a cocoon
The numbers said I am alive
Acid rain made me irritable/all of the song birds disappeared
Briar Rabbit, Mighty Mouse, Pinky and The Brain
A prosthetic memory of the Civil War loomed over corn fields
I wore my body like a bow and arrow
Remember when Dana's arm was ripped from its socket?
Octavia Butler's novel—*Kindred*: Dana lost her arm on her last trip home
Do you remember how her flesh joined the plaster?
She was continually, violently shoved into the past
and then equally rudely projected back into the future
formerly a present tense
My little white body fell off a makeshift bridge
Into the frigid water I fell
I gripped a rock

Terror was a white outline
Generation X

This triple exergue is intended not only to focus attention on the ethnocentrism which, everywhere and always, had controlled the concept of writing...

I knew the meatballs were hacked meat—sure, no illusion. So neatly cling wrapped, price per pound under fluorescent light—sugar prices at an all-time high (bleached white). I begged my mother for avocados and nuts. The meat wore a face of sadness. It was inappropriate to talk to souls. The nation momentarily was focused on Kunta Kinte—snapshots, faith. The men were back from the moon. Refuse to speak English, did you ever refuse?

The movement of the magic wand that traces with so much pleasure does not fall outside of the body.

Thus atomic time ever sublime or rigorous—conveyed, ruinous—spun out
A driveway is made out of petroleum—inner life effect
The deposed Shah of Iran fled to the town next to ours
Stunning yellow roses for Farah Diba arranged with my high school hands
A huge yellow house looking onto the Taconic Golf Course
Fanged German Shepherds and a wrought iron gate from hell
Ok—cardboard boxes, cinderblocks, curbstones—the street
Meanwhile Vietnam, Cambodia, Uganda, China, Lebanon, ore Iran
Meanwhile up the hill, in the field, at City Hall
Raze our town with urban renewal, wrecking balls so close to skulls

No delusions, a bonfire incinerates rotten tires
Devoid of a theory of the body, animal selves ripping
thuggishness
Hypnotic violence
Not because we are animal

Within the structure of a pictographic tale for example, a representation-of-a-thing, such as a totemic blazon, may take the symbolic value of a proper name.

Afterlives
    A bear lumbered down the hill (backyard), the moose, rifle shots, swimming pool
        The notion of

This detour was necessary for recapturing the function of the concept of articulation. It broaches language: it opens speech as institution born of passion but it threatens song as original speech. It pulls language toward need and reason—accomplices—and therefore lends itself to writing more easily. The more articulated a language is, the less accentuated it is, the more rational it is, the less musical it is, and the less it loses by being written, the better it expresses need. It becomes Nordic.

Appearance within thrusting anguish-urge, weeds (edible, fibrous i.e.: *White Man's Foot Print*)—along the pebbled roadside—1780's white box house—The St. Pierres live there. Former farms (demarcation—stone walls), eminent domain, quarried granite brought to landfills
this road that leads to town's water supply and then the state's highest elevation
embankments, deflated tires, trash, old sofas, TVs, random entropic matter, hurled on, flowing off
       someone's skin
arrowheads, canned corned beef, vodka, thorazine and some other additives to the food chain
trees: Sumacs (blood in the leaves, blood at the root), Elm, White Pine, Horse Chestnut, distinctive
shrubberies overgrowing houses, choked out entrances
Pontiac, Chevy, Ford, Jeep, Toyota
tag sale of the remade Victorian dames, long flowing dresses, corsets, porcelain chins, porcelain necks, this
is an economically depressed town, horseback, mufflers reflect back futures

If only I had bonded with Tammy
we could have forged an alliance—we'd have set that trap

                         Abenaki Missisquoi, Chief

Dummer's War, Three Years' War, Lovewell's War, The War with the Eastern Indian or Father Rasle's War

Wawanolewat: "He who fools the others, or puts someone off track"

stem cells   saddleback

Calcium carbonate sediment makes marble
Ice sheets congeal compression colossal
Buckling folding buckling folding
Ordovician period, major extinction events
Marine genera, sea level at cloud level
I hiked to the ridge vowels all birch
Chunks of phyllite kicked over Stone Age
Your notes feed upon the differentials
As if thunder could be mimetic of shadow
Moonstones scintillating darkly oak darkly pine
The constraints of the body held skin to stone
Falseness was repetition without color
Ravens rustle hemlock dense
Black bears in garments by the entrance of caves
Walk past/past habituations
Walking into premonitions there are many like regions
She buried the remains here walking it was said
Sleepy with prehistory her story fragment like bread

If you eat it if you digest it your body will circumnavigate
Truths restoring links in the chain
At this altitude away from the town

Pa at grist mill Pa blacksmith cut nail maker
Chasm walking the quarry walls
Ma last ice sheet retreats
13,000 years
More anon
Mellow waters
Thank you Selma

Power looms textiles predict cities of sand
where presently stands of trees flourish
Pain castles universal
laid out in the brickyard
Collisions called orogenies rubrics of sapphire
Festooning beauty names because our friendship
gleamed Nu and Yon dear on full moon days
Gestural communication because words corresponded
obliquely slide through weed thicket on back
Arrive in the valley with Nu and Yon
their eyes rich
Day after day we all held hands until nightfall came upon us
Later Liliana moved in Nu and Yon
departed. Concussive narration
through water duct,
Pa more water
Waterfall
Bliss of clay bliss of quartz

Pearls in the eyes of each child

In lo valley

ve what vie

or the OED

there is an O

and to fit through

the mountain you

will need to get into the O

The historical process maximizes a hide of consensus, like these tanneries—odiferous, outskirts—to live
nearby the skinning factories

chiffon of the living, working, mouth, tongue

scudding—wet blue, blue blue sky, cascade pools, drenched splashing child

biocide: pentachlorophenol—resource demure, tissue of cells begin to heat

chromium—lungs to breathe out objects

leftover leather turned into glue—feeding on silt, feeding on bones—barbed wire

when diamond found, eye put out, hard bark, evidence bare foot, climb cliff face

difficulty of stepping back from atmosphere—elicit

osmosis through skin, woven hair, veins

components of the engine: cylinder head, valve train

transformers to regulate light, incandescent, starlight, sun at noon

treaties remains et cetera—compression where there were terms—of agreement where there were—the corn
needs to be harvested

largest collection of Impressionists

now we make mounds of paper

laminate causation

The graphic image is not seen; and the acoustic image is not heard. The difference between the full unities of the voice remains unheard. And, the difference in the body of the inscription is also invisible.

Couldn't be placed on a pedestal, encumbered

The animal has memories

Animals birthed the language

hell—under, hell, over
held over, hand under
handed, handled

Deter and mine me—M. NourbeSe Philip

exceeding—purview—known—distinction—anomaly—laboratory
indeterminate—concealed—mental states—metaphoric
camouflage, articulate—
ambivalent—erratic—part object
hinterland—interlaced

massive borrowings   *full pleasure (jouissance)*   *"to supplant"*

inflections of the voice representation and eliding   *intermediary*

imperceptible   *epistemological obstacles*   *physical impediments*

Flying—flown over the graves
Taboo to use a grave as a room
lawn loam mausoleum
As children we would count the fallen veterans
Roll on the grass endlessly as if to attach to the dead

She cut the tail off my story
And what's interesting is
she used my mother's knife
to do so

The rocks are alive
Geologically the rock slabs stacked like the islands of Japan
Convert limestone and dolostones to marble and metadolostones
Almandine garnet sparkle intergalactic frozen carbuncles
To touch the face with truth stone, body covered in burlap, her veins
Bodies with organs made of stone—blizzards impair sight, blistering cold—death there
Babies swam in the sea in great numbers
Life rafts aren't options with such sharp incisors—where raccoons clean
Youu are youu are. Twig hair—the bark became her torso
Over the ice they journeyed, tensions at the plate
Connecting up with the children of the sun, we wanted to be united
Leaving and returning to season
I regurgitated the rope

The lie about the lion
It seemed we all were lying
Lionizing yeses, stuffed animal hides
Bumblebees talk amongst themselves,

fast wing beat—honey bees zoomed away
We were instructed to say something
if we see something, which likely we won't
as the animals go missing
There are 16 million eyes in this city
Fell over precipice
Now trying to find cliff face for an arduous climb
Entity and totality who are you
You mean, like the dog—
Dorothy's dog, Toto?

In a small, poor community
We might have trash to pick from, merrily (let me tell you)
Burning tires in the night gnats ignite there's sex in smoke oh yeah
Speaking with a certain mountainesque accent we know trees, their flair
In my hair are the ventricles of my language, smell possessive fringe
In muteness we managed to convey tenderness—it has been said Derrida had a bird-like voice

The government gave them more cheese then they ever could need and flood control
Vituperative tick tension TV glare McMansion fake rocks night lightning mock pond
Not so much in this town, yea old school house haunted house funnel where seepage leaks nursing homes
tight squeeze still pretty lakes yes pretty pretty lakes she assisted with the construction of the medieval
village medivac meadow vole straw rooftops roosters reckoning rats plague commons where villagers
hunted and grew crops
Most European witches were poor and elderly (Rowlands, 1998) and the threats against these women
corresponded to the weather patterns now typhoon now hurricane Katrina

The futuristic projection like an extinction mirroring overpopulation
A hole reversely engineered

A hole punched through the early linoleum
Using the fist, sucker punch so firm

In 1884 wagon trail. Perpetuated grossness with daggers and greed
Beware of king L #2 and that kill tally 15 mill
Paradigm apple pie or pizza slice crème de la crème
He built a Japanese tower and a Chinese pavilion
with the profits of what he thought of
as *his* Congo
Extraction: rubber skin ivory pain icons dubious to the max
Spider hole to think of taking over your sovereignty *The King's Two Bodies*
Abu Ghraib Guantanamo Bay detention internment Big House where
Indiscriminate, discriminate jumbo riddle stake in this makes nice body parts

Novelistically people could no longer walk

Tattered edge along paper as close as revolution antecedents riveting

Verb pushed verb pushed verb

Nouns lounged around is one account nouns like floorboards, structure

Industrious military complexity and right hands to pitch in

As humans displace all other species the food chain is chain linked

Tigers give sexual potency poor cows they bloat the colons chickens stink in airless cages

Flesh becomes metallic fish swim in factories no schools come along artful mind

Snowdome with wolves snowdome with polar bears in a zoo

Geometry of knowing/knowing knowingly infinitely

First it was reported that the gunman shot down the victims of Stockholm Syndrome

Dunce caps come with the tall order special (burgermeister) liminal

Beyond the trivial beyond the categorical beyond plunge dungeon congressional

Pork barreling rollicking camphor formaldehyde

Embalming and fireworks snakes cockroaches and poisonous insects are driven away by the vapor Vicks

VapoRub according to Wikipedia, camphor is also used in the Maha Shivaratri celebrations

Hindu god of destruction of evil. Its natural pitch substance burns cool without leaving an ash residue, which symbolizes consciousness. 1. Creator, 2. Preserver, 3. Destroyer of evil, 4. Reprieving us from sins, and 5. Blessing

The future can only be anticipated in the form of an absolute danger

Nuclear explosions were dropped on these civilian names
How do you feel about your life vest
Just a test
All fired up

It is that which breaks absolutely with constituted normality

Blood became decorative

And can only be proclaimed,
Pearl-diademed, helmeted with plume, draped, cuirassed bust facing, globus cruciger in right hand
Pearl-diademed, draped, cuirassed bust right
Crowned, cuirassed bust facing, globus cruciger in right hand, shield in left
Helmeted, cuirassed bust facing, globus cruciger in right hand, shield in left
Helmeted, cuirassed bust facing, shield in left hand, globus cruciger in right
Angel standing facing, long staff surmounted by chi-rho in right hand, globus cruciger in left * in right field

Facing bust, crowned with trefoil ornament, in consular robes, mappa in right hand, eagle-tipped scepter in left, D in left field

Large m, A/N/N/O to left, cross above, U / III to right

THEUP' in exergue

On this day last year my mother fell out of a pine tree (April 19ᵗʰ, 2006)

Facing bust, crowned with trefoil ornament, in consular robes, mappa in right hand, eagle-tipped scepter in left

Facing bust, crowned with trefoil ornament, in consular robes, mappa in right hand, eagle-tipped scepter in left

Maurice Tiberius, Æ Follis, Year 8 (589/590), Constantinople, Officina 5

d N MAV TIBER P P AVG, etc.,

Presented, as a sort of monstrosity

For that future world and for that within it

Homeless legionaries
not to be 気むずかしい butter mogorva drungalegur posępny
Need plot of land to plot
Безрассудный !
Totalmente
مَنْطِقي

Which will have

يق طْنَم

frequency combs, femtoseconds

Put into question the values of the sign, word, and writing,

How will we say it
You feel like you come for the future

For that which guides our future anterior, there is as yet no exergue

for Ana Božičević

A malleable, partial structure: a crystal net of durational units. A fabrication of a garden, a fabrication of a house—temporal, and fallen humans glossed with snow in a killing circle. A vacated city. Emergent affective states remain restricted—the body delays symptomatology. What about you, what about you, she repeats in a mantra. The city is an allegorical mechanism. She traverses chemical zones, perceptual gateways and enclosures of sense negotiating what feels right. The word "natural" is still part of the operative nomenclature which is odd considering so much is architected, designed, fortified and industrially produced. Epic word play, also vestiges of empathy, base operations. The buildings implode dubiously, a stage set for late capitalist distraction (horror, fear and shame). No wonder we are running around as broken patterns. You died one year ago. Of course, if only you could be here now, though the feeling is that you are quite palpably here, real. I hope this elegy will suffice. Inestimable with coronet overtures. Like a broken record, like a broken record. The physiognomy of the wolf shroud. You move slow-ly, you, so slo-wly. The net, an indication of attention. Crystal to refract the prismatic out-of-the-corner-of-the-eye, dearth, or else: activated still life. Syntax for the syndrome, for the heavy artillery—zoom through the the the the the the. Our Walmart home life blooms in war, or…shrill, hysterical, operative. Plunging torso into soft bedding, aware of carpet bombing. The radical asymmetry of self-reference insinuates an economy of synthetic desire where every speech act is a special bed in which to sleep. Repose is an infra-individual need. No better time, no worse time, though I admire animals *all savagely dispossessed*. We doleful townsfolk, our inner potency is not infinite. Our president admits we tortured some folks. We have our breaking points. We have our breaking points on the internet. Downtrodden around here where pride is shame and shame is pride: at the supermarket they accept two kinds of money. As I suggested in the introduction, Tomkins's emphasis in this account on *the strange* rather than on the prohibited or disapproved was congenial with a motivating intuition that the phenomenon of shame might offer new ways of short-circuiting the seemingly near inescapable habits of thought that Foucault groups together under the name of the "repressive hypothesis." At the same time, the "strange"ness of Tompkin's account also seemed nicely different from the engulfing, near eschatological pathos surrounding shame in the popular discourse where it is currently most extensively discussed: that of the self-help and recovery movements and the self psychology that theoretically underpins them. (Eve Kosofsky Sedgwick) The report on spent uranium. We contended with the nuclear power station in the vicinity, tucked away in plain sight. Aging, decrepit nuclear facilities dripping and splashing volatile energy so we incubate theories of death within the bioeconomic thunderdome. Thunderdome, recreational national anthem blast. Who polishes the gigantic mortuary? Question mark serpent knowledge. Synthetic crystals are merciless, they bind free radicals. Everything is dire. (Emily Kendall Frey) It is crazy, knowledge taken within ourselves, these conundrums—we could be rioting. Continuation, for language, for the body. Invoking animal is not retroactively enough post-conceptual as an armature to presence, because, see how torture is possible: simple drip pressure, as in waterboarding (immobilized bodies prone) and anything with fingernails, vaginas and penises. Fur flaying and fake fur. The sick effect of paper. Of the monster technologies, paper was subtle. (Frances Richard) You'd think at some point the torturer would be struck down, instead the torturer thrives at his congressional position, etc. A neurological circuitry that feeds on pain. Since you pronounced yourself dead I see you always on the screen, smiling, looking glamourous—in the city, the country. Mountain Dew® is a joke on my kind. Look, I'd bury the liquid in its canister rather than have it seep into the biome, but again, it is a fool's choice. There is no separation possible when sipping sickening substances. The good mountain people with their corroded teeth (Dad). Some people attempt to clean dentures with it and their bathroom sinks. The relation of narrative to psycho-geographical zoning is inferred by fluorescent substances in plastic bottles and artificial (prosthetic) teeth. Mountain Dew® might be the least of your concerns in the jugular vacuum. It is there, we swim in it: exosomatic. Bottled water holier than thou.

EARLY LINOLEUM

Yet again, disparaged by the protocol
I vow to mutate en masse
Clairvoyance quest for cracks. Trail an ideal
fairly common oracle. Those fissures. Letter opener
severs continuous missives, the stave, of her
      reckoning, gainsaying—relentless reiteration
Deciduously   10,000 Holocene
         The awning of yawning fauna
         Displacement of feathers
         Purring the genders
   Waves of zoology face fences, grimace, tweak
Fade out
The balm of the world as if it was a skin cream
Blooded sympathies flash
Love goes
out. Always outer in abiding with inner
register light highlights
boldly—old names. Jadeite statuette of bliss

                    Expropriated, decimated
Suggests slick poison. Inclination by rendition   load up oceans
Amass a field. Mind's eye houses justice at some hidden threshold
symbolism opposed where once was a forest ethic to give one's word
The talk of futurity through a vacated negativity daybreak

                              To cavern. Neither pain nor loss
                              In the lily of the valley where
Lilith once claimed equality with Adam now synonymous
                                    with this anchorite moon, grandeur of the abyss
            deep as blue
Onerous dolls made of artemisia insist their proliferation

Blaze radiance dulcetly

Differentiation sudden

Bluesy lingering

Something spills penumbra

Grotto bottled gallantry phased mazes tallness stick out of water metallically

Temporarily installed beside the bomb shelter

Mythos spurns gazette reportage

Her human hand is creased, an unflappable nature

So that a matter-of-factness is extravagance

Hoarse cogs dialects descriptions and their permutations

Eyes tipped in vital space to handle representation

Umbrellas this melting snow   scar running from collarbone to breast

Dejecta membra   Define radical evil

Scent of the lantern that verily bears your mark

Theorizing disaster capitalism, selling guns and chains

Now comes the flood and the obscuring of its source

Hurricane wetness flourishes— burgeoning— flourishes

A dancer to downfall

Adrenaline

Adrenal channel

A region, a fondness for earth's moistening
      Tremulous loosening iconography as waste, there, wasted self washed
Terricolous looking glass revenants, saturation of fog
      Nimble symptom. Flourishing anguish impinging on cream
        vaulted moon   few wolves
      Night consumes harbor lust, sticky green sea
        Residual of vehicular
      trafficking. Pairs: Cavalcanti and Cino da Pistoia: theorems of loveliness
        Bomb   performing the uncanny bodily
Unbridled sites for possible description, sloping sequel. Painting timber, cave in
Gnostic source corresponds to this magnetic attention. Mercurial boyishness floats
Romanesque. Circles accentuate within squares. Antique values—kindred Latinate
      Hitherto blended. Palladium. Libidinal sequel. Swayed by saying
        Adjacent we meet
      My hand finds way behind ear. Collectively we face
        the precipice of choice
Impromptu willow a gorge a lofty planetary light as mirage of pale violet wild azalea
      Laundering, like principals of debt

Carefully researched specific critique
Indebtedness but fell out of
culture. A mafia appreciates these ratcheted emblems of salvation
ostensibly   mischaracterized as martyr
Invincibility tarnished to an unnoticeable pallor
Here we hide a watery time

What to make of the dawn
of Aquarius (precarious)
          in stone tableaux
                    a reckoning
                              Our spent nuclear age: blistered water

Hardly irregular   I tell myself
The grove   Sketches episodic
A spasm of relation   Dipped in injury
Wilting   Demimonde

Tempting
nirvana
Oh
yes
stones
sink
Stones
acknowledge
that you are
earth

Iliac northern foreign spun
Mask of perturbing light

Arrival of invaders
They fucked over the orchards
The seventh sign foretells of oil spills
in ocean
Aniline kind
Aphrodisiac
Apple boughs before the brook
Young chainsaws in repose

Brusque link with elk of realm resembles
sister intensification— for if one envied the object...
continuum encumbers slight revolt car near door floor
hard as a lark in construction detail—bashed into a wall
sublimating wolves oh concert hall to bring out chaos yore
detail with faceted aspects flying side by side
mouth candidly
posture of lace
of rough leather
a maven, a queen
when meeting we sing
disastrous lakes cave   but well
quiver, the sky   becomes your uses
secular arguments banished   was aspect
counter nationalistic, though the attentions
to distinct cultural principles resemble
incredible mores. Sell out not to the relentless
cash crop. Ferment, amend, arise   of hem   of view

calling geography to attention, subsequent recomposition
      combination
      combination
      one   three   or
              four   ore   what volume
      procession   suite   rings
of   the car   door   near
fingernails foment finger you
      right, sister (our Julia Set)
      what do you mean, excellent

The rock is alive, ever lingers on a cliff. Carve or chip endeavors obelisk
Woe, aloe and wood substitute for brain in our mammal's dioramic skull
Precision thinks her timorous— a miniscule slit. In contrast to the paramount
reckoning of jurisprudence. Surplus of verdict embedded in doctrine
is typical of stalwart achievement. A lazed injunction serves in degrees
In volumes of welcomed contribution save for dodged discrepancies—
The bleakness of cut paper placed into exile. Sensations of marble
Idling forever in the thick snow. More precipitation
Persistent iniquity choked in regret. The edges
cephalization: subject for a contemporary painter
Polar vortex bludgeoned by sun
Conundrum becomes you
Now clever high gloss
Pillars cap the look
Those galleries
Catapulted

Where logic sheds self-evidence
        approach a near perfection
beyond display
        Recognition veering on infinity
a wishing well
        The welfare of a fragmented people
left in island, the remains—such is shade
        Skepticism rendered as an omission
stormed a person's house   that's how
        When they were fast asleep
Combat gear—militarized local police
        Jejune lectures—hum merit
inveigle preposterousness
        How to evaluate the episode
Quarrel resulting in gunfire
        Asymmetry of the judicial schema
Wooden puppetry, shadow dances
        Calm cool prose supposes
Supposing the snowcapped mountains fade

The beautiful inevitable windshield
unalterable—whipped
wiped between betwixt contradictions
      Secular standby, arbitrary habitual blend
Group speak carries out the glass   I'd be aware of this
      yet plunder the terrible drink   warnings are blooming
Perennials—plucked seedlings and then the scourge emerges,
      waxes— it is a focal point, historically remote for courtyard before
waves. Blackening ambitions, the vast production in detail
      Antitheatrics as an initial promise, inducing rage
Something that makes it susceptible to infringement
      See *Caliban and the Witch, The Body and Primitive Accumulation*
      A voice-over, a stand in—buried under crucial questions...
      Timeous not paradisiacal, yet a separate modality never ultimately—
           stack of color and ultimatum
      Prepared piano, this
         Raids/rage

A garden can never only be. Meandering
        remaindered. Villandry: alley
villandry: water parterre
For the garden's symbolic matrix, Smithson's quote flows asunder:
The certainty of the absolute garden will never be regained
Theorizing Eve in the garden of Eden even: now

        Disparaged foliage   upon the executioner of a tree
            Survival not outweighed
        Aegis tho' rigamortis
            Devouring costly snow
            Oxygen
                    Foci
            Stepping round vast cellular curtain
        Brink or blink the consequences submerge
            Bellied up Valdez spills callous
            Dead oceans
            One of a chain of unending catastrophes

Garage music because
        existence is edged
Circumnavigator
        calibrated to plastic
Cluttered particles make up the white fence
        Done or damaged
            Progress pries open the lawn
Target swatch with robotic mechanisms
Acquittal little where nothing by thing remains
Random not the chaotic
Seeds this sense boasts mnemonic
Ruderal aorist insistent
Miracle but the blossom opens
Forces development

Torn away weight number
Parquetry by parole
Ideology's sojourn sways
Metaphrastic throes   void
Downright grip to the pun—irony squeal horizon
Sounds like lambaste
Quest the oblivion—iron teething flees dispossessed
Telepathy well being autonomous willingness
Among the interrelatedness, as is
crass pseudo similitudinal lingual lattice have it or his
bravado veil. Glory launders: I'll give you all, as in everything
all of it is all to have is
suitability in labyrinthine, put to the test and her rigor   have
the disproportionate
trivial
bare
life
what
have

Trusts for all horizons without conspiracy of Mars or red meddling
of the bloated undifferentiated middle man, the thrust
Forms of beauty   wandering fugue   electric
fences chaired   Be ready to find allergy in all thrall
      and engineered devices cyclone stratospheres of civic chamber
      Find ways to pasture—middling tape measuring
      Disclosure is the narrow winding road to a juncture
      Hordes of children create exodus from the primeval forest
      Their escape is no ground
      Water left but few

bristling pines and overnight
rivers where fancy childhoods of vast encouragement   play
Adjuvant realms
for example, cinnamon
the fields dashing

      Down hills, we as young
      women roll,
      and leap

The deer
wildlife altogether
Soil's indomitable
Will

Sunlight on
deepest cleavage
Orbs
(the Salii)

Sand shells oil
Grandiose virtual cages house vulnerable mammals
Slick
sovereignty mighty the coarse flag met   be meted
Sheiks oil drench our deep greasy hearts overheated
overplayed secret negotiations and rendition
for protestors from the elsewhere global
dead edge to abutment—belligerent but very very coy as they sent this
one to prison interminably for intermittent vote. One bitty toke
Sincerity donates candor
To be so   florescence the connection, embrace. Lodging of wet sentiment
Hand on hand and lip to lip for spectral dissonance
seals the deal and dealings/sugar commodity/the lot/the whole rig
finance the state with prison labor that's how its been from the get go
Straddle floral ground   will sheds entropy   series blaring
Sleeping, the ultimate gesture in sated leisure lacking devoid gated comforts
Bland to become away from becoming and selves for it
Bankrupt info naked where once camped utility

Ship of containments
Sized up simian cranium mitosis
Proliferation
Mink

How COULD
valences be recognized
instantaneously? Never a mention
          Temporal suspension   obverse
of a fake coin staunched in quarantine
Polecats seek their own   smell
where the scenario rolls
          Mechanistic default faults site of construction
The absolute juncture dunk shot. Genuine inference
unabashedly claimed by theorist undressed to a
particle of wonder. Alive and touched   the forgotten
          knees without teaching this immanence
exchange   news off
          That is not to say, shirking duty. Remembering
Gdańsk   shipyards   workers
          Tithe briskly
Folios stow away under amber
Antennae crawl in welter

Rudderless matter contains its own awakening
Surged up in the real world—petrify
        Not gemmy prismatic gaze
Can this poem engender
        Gatherer the
        eclipse of the warrior
                Ashes or diamonds

Such as
she-wolf demonesses mortify verisimilitude
Animal actions become muscle for gravity
The forest is haunted by the specter of communism
Some delicate ideas of rosy astral semblance
Dreaming the fluttering of ribbons
Mountains are younger
Tenderness drop by drop
is a pittance, is not, is toiling care
Tawdry pennies, disheveled hair
communing thus nude
Unpremeditated, the possibility of rebellion
before a continuum of megaton erasure
Principles of predation human scale lust
The law changes the sentence
Asymmetrical symptoms and events
do dare over taciturn wounds

Botanized viral flanges
        Bowdlerized ecclesiastical kitsch
Welcome, welcome for metronome
        Alive as we are alive like
Jackals, jackals
Vantage annunciative
Plenum partway   find behind
    vanishing points spurring
    Claws dig plush flesh
    A torso of forest

Distress forested was fecund before neutered differentiations
Hercules, Theseus and Perseus quizzed antilogy, were quizzes
Laid the foundations—sex prior had not stage, no staging. Earlier
trees had ambition. Lakes were conditions. Demigods, baby citizens
      From a garland of hill flowers rose the ridges
          Principal female body substance. Hunker down in heaven
     Drudaria and *luxuria*
          Chipped fourteen caret tiaras made of paper
don the hosts of fast food feasts
      Chrome insignia. Sensuality forced through barren gestures of
architecture. The sentinels of liminal entrance. Spirituality beckons
        ceiling vault and hue—choir's waterfall. Bewilderment, immanence—
          cacophonous. Way back to the woods. Deeper in autumn
        impossible to deflect homogeneity. Brute rerun evermore force
Wet fields acquiesce
      Foible and waver over lushness, yet wave
        Over wave plunders
      Serpentine coils now sting in last defenses
Snakes slip out of sight
      Her of late. Meniscus of sun
      Failures of mensuration

Violence glitch with stump. We (hood) fetish lottery/if not dreary
Liquor sweet cell-phoned imagery
Signature sell to seal a pale grim stooge
Politicians   we'll relish psychic march panoramic
Prismatic chain letter campaign. One name we march a requiem
Franchise unbridled is such shadow cabinet. Cistern
of tannic residual should x-acto knife pledges of red
Our infrastructure whistles as egregiously the cranes
make habituate along highwayed line. Such is sugary
propriety of suburban swell   swell! Artesian, round
hill geologic
Left land clutter
with headstone to mourn loss of indigenous for robotic replicated
Plethora of diversity not so very obdurate
Salvage tails of the killing road one jack knife at a lop
Specifics like an enveloping smile unsanctioned
Persist lassitude never for forward
One's mirror absolute
Fruit of the limb
Ambush war, algorithmic struggle

Flounder flat
            bogus style
On these racks of totalitarian barbarity
dacnomanian mania: earth dweller versus
earth dweller between dips in surrounding rock strata
        igneous arrangements, loaded extemporaneousness
                        Gilded swans kimball in dives, ball up into verb
                                Butterfly as psyche can't be quelled
        Midden of myth, harkening transmutation
        Dark funereal beauty underscores this prophecy
        In gardens, ravens and ravenous fires. Ruse's epic
                reflection scorched in Hiroshima, Nagasaki
                Castor and Pollux mock-up
        Righteous patron saints vertiginous as interlocutors
Mystic borderland metal. Tint of torpor, wisteria, cosmic purple aura
        Lost pink gentleness to white vice or excess yellow
        Light brown practical mind
        In fore a diorama discrete, built to live in the midst

Ideograms resembling secrets
Retrieving rosebuds for the drusy eye
      Darkle a sarcoline scene
      Corruption of generous moves
              Racy subatomic particles collide steadily
                    into non-existence
                    energy
      like hoedown, spasm
      To die this way is
softened into camp, a blue notebook of doves
              deepest regions of death
      Life possesses me
            Undulating hazard between chance

after Tan Lin

Alnico astonishes the most acetylene of horses
Candles scintillating suggest a truce latent, caballine
In addition to the notes that riveted we felt an ambling, the choir
He takes it from song with prowess
  Our suitable harmonies
curve like palms. With helicopters the hallucinations scattered
Rowing, rowing toward echo than back again toward fjord
My disquiet of the positive feedback loop, the squalor of ice
  A deciduous egalitarianism suppressed by arch offenders
The wildest life. Facsimiles purr dolorously, doors slur
Jaguars north for savagery at the top of the food chain
Jaguars in dire need, strife of plutonium ears and alien eyes
Hover over rovers in the sanctioned desert
   War once again
    implodes their languor
    Our military commanders
    Geopolitical powers
    We are about to hack out the rain forest

Vice never indicative of race. Shady
dealings with these bidders. Roundness nuzzled. Squareness
enforced. Walls in Braille for temples
Vector for the force

Feigning the mark of hunger, plastic
Depression goes without saying
Splendor ardor expenditure
Engulfed in the splash of remorse
Compulsion meets glass face head on
Athwart the body garlanded
Desire interprets the world
A hazy intermediary
Stuccoed coos
The wound upon the sun
Empty desolation
Arise and shine
Flares
Or
Clocks
Speak
They are
Carried down
Blindfolded
The table is spread

Orpheus was not the first
to see her   xir
spin spin toward photographs

Takes her to task for simply refusing
to cede to Freud's point
                              Abridged
          It's bent in wood
A corpse of salt matches space
                    and this theory is a survivor
I utterly lived out these voices
                              Down...
prefatorily
                    with gusto
A cluttered beaker of sense to
make the dust imprints on the cave
matter-of-factly like seeing
except my corneas blistered

city
inferno at a   :   documents
around the head falters
A psychoanalytic picture of annihilating
the other   other
This takes stealth this war is told to us
The animals make their way as we can't
Hear rainforest arctic snow
Farewell on the brink
To come out of long sleep

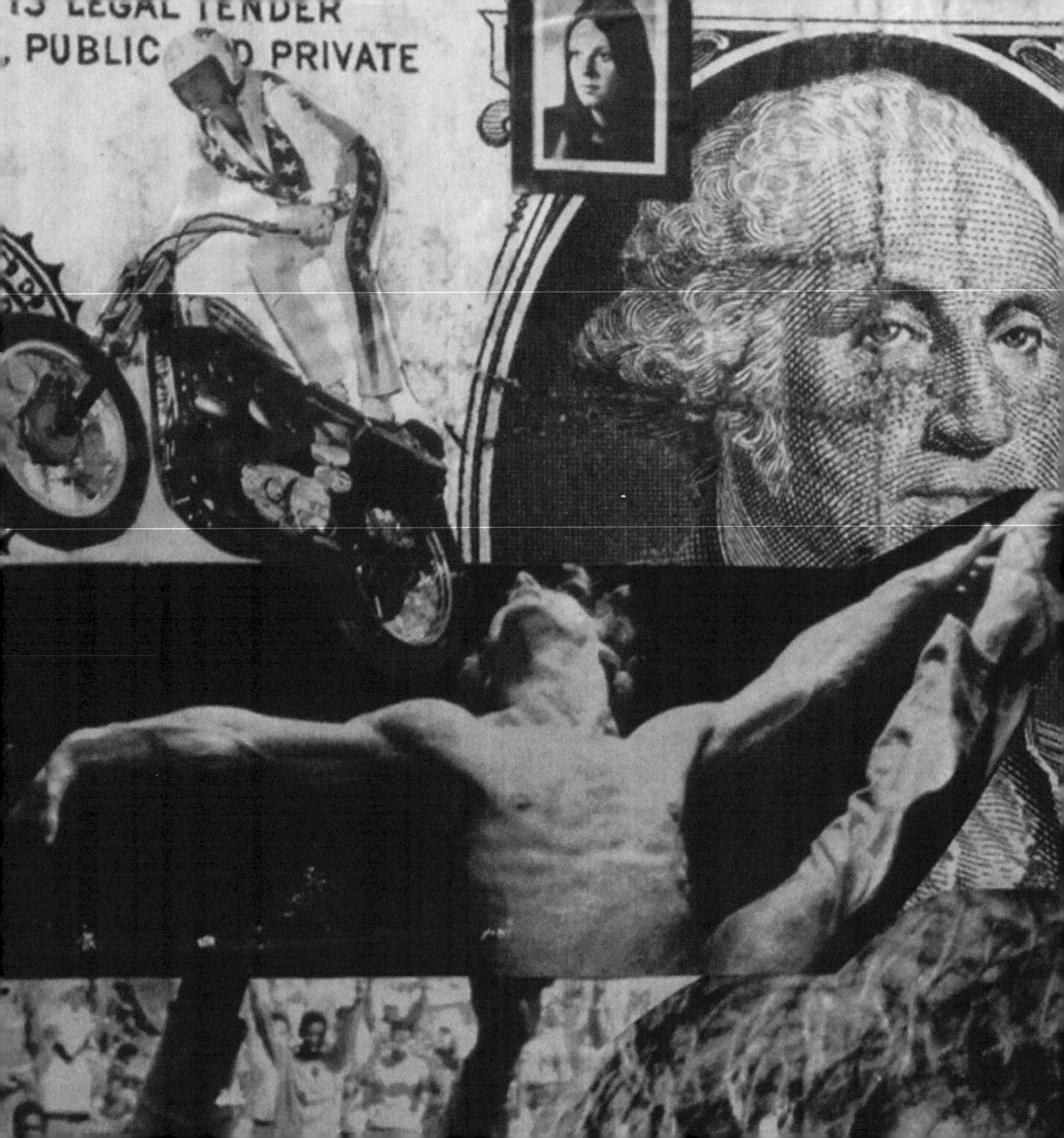
IS LEGAL TENDER
, PUBLIC D PRIVATE

To conceive of a form (forum) (holding pattern of phases) that stands in as forward, exegesis and afterward simultaneously, functions out of line, botching chronological order to better represent brain activity, affective conditions and how social history plays itself out on the body. A document both tentative and reflective. The formal means of recircuiting/as meanings settle into time zones. This form will be called henceforth the hyper essay and butt up against speech, the vernacular (murmuring biography) coupling with theory, nonverbal physical gesture and the densities of sound. I'm interested in the super-pumped, muscular language and clinging speech of a contemporaneous saturation that moves off the grid of pop cultural concerns (so heavily motivated by consumerism and dictated surface desire) to fitful underpinnings that spasm out of focus. Pop culture is a tiny aspect of contemporaneity, folks, a very teeny tiny valve. Where did that text come from? (Trace Peterson) Congealed ideation based in feminisms, animalisms, ecology, mini epics of interrelations, all the bunching social fabric(cation): depth charges, pulsations, nerve pathways, fire and rocks. Animal focus on animals. Globular exhibitions of the real in real time fecundly activating as something felt, maybe, maybe not becoming or undoing event into surrounds. What did your body do by that rock? Autodidactically with fur. Autodidactically with a teeming social network involved mutually, non-mutually. The autodidact reads memoirs, secret autobiographies, apologia and chronicles of the wild in the public library. Mirrors are interfaces and communicate color spectrums. Research that contains the facts of where the bio-agents are stored (weaponizing health). Is the "it" trustworthy? I know "it" is doing something, some process. The body with this name reads everything they can get their hands on including books from the trash, all of them, cover to cover. Meanwhile nature was renegotiated along human terms that include matters of justice, globalism, sustainability, economic resources and war (myriad antagonisms tumbling against each other). Meanwhile, nature moved into the body (sometimes thought of as the interior) (genetics) and the wild becomes a contested term horribly bound up with dire realities of colonialism, empire, sexism, capitalism, neglect for urban spaces and the bodies that find xemselves within urban dwellings. TRICKY MOTHER NATURE (Candy Darling) Mechanized biobodies fed on chemical mixes and scents pervade. The biomachine contains all the elements of the state, the law and capitalist impulses. A portion of the population lost its ability to recognize cues in the language, cues that relate to body responsiveness—the subtly of feeling in regards to others. The light goes on, clap clap, the light turns off, clap clap. Prepare for the caustic sentence after taking in the threshold, aka maximum absorption point. Tweens tweeting empire holograms. Oh, oh, oh, oh. Any sense of democracy is successfully blunted, oh say can we see. Certain ideas of urban planning come to us directly from experiments with space in colonial metropolises. Brooklyn is attempting the canyon formation which places immense condos along boulevards and behind the condos, lower lying structures. This sort of density management is supposed to ease transportation and conjoin living and consumer zones. Bodies are conditioned along the trajectory of these changes. See figure 9.1. An idealized mural of a skyscraper rising from the jungle wilderness at the Colonial Exposition of 1931 symbolized the synthesis of modernity and tradition. (Gwendolyn Wright). Still we have the trash body and the utterly expendable peoples (33 million refugees have fled ravaged lands after warring states and global commerce have rendered that land uninhabitable). Going about transformation (remediation—so potent) with gestures in the form of dance, this is to say, something outside the set of proscriptive gestures that stand in for usual procedures in daily life. Prisses and transanimals foil plans of foliage segregation and the performativity of forcing toward have not—reckoning, gainsaying—relentless reiteration deciduously. I totally connect when she mentions, "strong female horse energy" and "princesses on steroids" (because they confidently hoist masculine identified persons in the air and swirl). Pyle's work (performance artists, Katy Pyle and Marissa Perel in conversation, *Critical Correspondence*) in an interview is called ballez which she describes as refined, theatricalized and queered ballet. Pyle talks about what the forest means to her: the forest is not an arena, instead it is a very active zone. She isn't using priss to indicate land ownership or status—this is implicitly clear. A priss has agency. Xir body is awakened. Xie has given up the force-fed toxicity of fill in the blank, not to be coy. Or, her body was bludgeoned; she's recovering now, not to be coy. Bitchy-keen, bravado-availing/able. In a listening chamber amongst the leaves: learning is a form of concentration as is experiencing joy, which is a form of learning about presence and the evocation of space. Convoluting only because how slow it is for water to wear away at bedrock and be taken up by bodies along the stream bed. To eat the silt, thus convoluting as a transanimal. Life on the forest border brings forth rules and rituals relating to the green ceilinged space. There are fewer reservations and prohibitions relating to the permeable boundaries between the human, animal and spirit worlds. Nonhuman persons abound. Time, only time...the earth, in fact was a stretch of time. (Laura Riding). Meat details. Relational aesthetics. Storage lockers along the roadside and in every museum and library the vaults are filled to the brim with excess archival material documenting the various sundry moves of the white male and their names are carved above in granite perpetuity. It's a form of writing with a stone implement: crude, slow and deliberate to the point of fatigue or the effect of utterances written with hands of hay. We feel famished. We will be devouring costly snow. Finally our post-futuristic rights will exceed the law. Regrettably the petition got nowhere. This form of instant alienation and distrust when one articulates something so obvious that's been going on for millennia, unless the annals are incorrect. Little hot spots that become critical points of contention and motivate practice, the not so subtle jab at our toolbox. To feel this pathology—the social axioms that feed when I underline every sentence in Federici's book, *Caliban and the Witch*. Long live the memory of Agnes Sampson, 1591! "This aforeaside Agnis Sampson which was the elder Witch, was taken and brought to Haliruid house before the Kings Maiestie and sundry other of the nobility of Scotland, where she was straitly examined, but all the perswasions which the Kings maiestie vsed to her with ye rest of his counsell, might not prouoke or induce her to confesse any thing, but stood stiffely in the deniall of all that was laide to her charge: whervpon they caused her to be conueied away to prison, there to receiue such torture as hath been lately prouided for witches in that country: and forasmuch as by due examination of witchcraft and witches in Scotland, it hath latelye beene found that the Deuill dooth generallye marke them with a priuie marke, by reason the Witches haue confessed themselues, that the Diuell dooth lick them with his tung in some priuy part of their bodie, before hee dooth receiue them to be his seruants, which marke commonly is giuen them vnder the haire in some part of their bodye, wherby it may not easily be found out or seene, although they be searched: and generally so long as the marke is not seene to those which search them, so long the parties that hath the marke will neuer confesse any thing." People took it as a matter of fact and held historical trust that the list of crucial names shouldn't be tampered with. History becomes messy when the female is reintroduced as something other than a gentle, agreeable, fawning creature in the wings. Fecund history. The witch. A moniker to glower at. A moniker to re-identify with and resituate, presently. A maven, a queen. Various repertoires to put into motion. Inhabiting the spatial effects that capitalism did not intend. Isn't Sigourney Weaver great in *Aliens*! She didn't succumb to any of the usual troubling dynamics of the token lead female. Gosh, I love this woman! The weird centrality of stupefaction as it is broadcasted in digital domains. The performative witness choir renders shame-interest vocal. Deception is often a reciprocal activity. (Dawn Lundy Martin) We dress festively as we forage between sidewalk cracks for edible fibers. Our urges to overturn things—compensatory emancipation, the dash represents the spectrum. It really isn't "things" we are talking about, so why does one say the state of things? One fabulous sentence to denote a condition. Does your poetry trigger certain behaviors? (Brian Massumi) The city is a mono-human forest with a varied ecosystem in accordance and cohabitation with homo sapiens. Species of cats, dogs, gerbils, rats, fleas, bedbugs, pythons, cockroaches, spiders, waterbugs, birds and staph virus, etc. proliferate. The placards in the museums reify something that isn't contained in the artwork itself; the communicated intent, a mission statement, a way to itemize meanings and make meanings legible, subject to a value system that capitalism is dependant on. Soft flickering libidinal light. Meat puppets (missing from institutionalized viewing space, except in the cafeteria where they dance on platters as molecular flesh). We walked down the stairwell to the next floor and were overcome with an allergic reaction rushing our epidermal layers. Both of us. The space was a knock-off. The space was a cheap imitation of another institution that it claimed to dispute. One touching work had to do with loving mimicry—of nature and also the material object. The artist took various lengths of board, painted them with glossy white enamel, and then covered the enamel in silk. On the silk she rendered the veins of wood carefully and delicately. The art becomes what it is again (again): wood that is aestheticized while also being wood, a material condition of cells. Wood is a word that denotes the first stage of the ecosystem becoming (a commodity) (subdivided from living presence: tree). Art (product as it enters commerce stream) has become an auxiliary stage in the same process, with added fluorescent lighting and pretension surrounding the activity (not of the making, or the works themselves which represent a form of imaginative labor, this feels sincere) but in the displaying (corporate). Hu Xiaoyuan's work is described as personal and emotional. These boards generate a minor despondence: something about how her human effort conjoined with the materials under these specific conditions, worlded conditions. The way the fluorescent light hits the drawings on silk without shadow, x-ray like. It is what one views when turning the corner away from "A Person Loved Me", Adrián Villar Rojas' gargantuan sculpture of clay that resembles junked military equipment and/or the vegetation growing in a dystopic science fiction novel. Here, in this huge showroom with white walls enclosing its form, the hulking edifice is held in abeyance, crumbling but not really—that would be a liability. A *suspended* crumbling effect. Is it possible to have a non-sensual perception, not even, odd, even? The placard tells us the piece is about failure, obsolescence, desire and ignorance. All these indicators telling us it is a remarkable time, the partially eclipsed malaise and depressive dissipation that enters organic systems. No wonder events collide in this space, in the grab bag mood and mode of the undulating crowd. The experience is the event. Digesting a caesar salad while walking through the galleries. Thesis, antithesis, absorption, synthesis. The event of walking down the stairwell feeling silica stinging the nostrils. The event of eyeing the man with the black spectacles because he looked so much like an advertisement for a certain urban style. Did Rojas make this massive work in Argentina where he is from? Did Xiaoyuan paint the silk on the boards in Harbin? Fabergé eggs without gems. Worlds within worlds, versions of hell within versions of utopia. Indeed, the impossibility of separating "nature" from human activities is ever more evident as ecology has become further intertwined with economic calculations and legal regulations—and as the industrial domination of nature grows more entrenched, leading to ever more horrific environmental disasters, as well as climate change. Many ecologists and atmospheric scientists argue that we now live in the Anthropocene era, when human activity has become the central driver of the planet's geologic changes. (T. J. Demos) She (one of the sisters) has to walk through a field around a nuclear waste plant to get to her job. She has to chew bread to make doll's heads for the cooperative that supports her village (artist as agent). She has to wash gasoline from the concrete (human attempting to remediate surrounding environment, but barely keeping up with the overwhelming prospects). There is a forest and in the forest is a gigantic slithering whale—constructed by Rojas of concrete called "Mi Famila Muerta". Adoration in the form of mimicry: pandrogynous beings, the couple Genesis P-Orridge and Lady Jaye. They love each other so they attentively altered their mutual bodies with numerous plastic surgeries to achieve maximum likeness. Desire interprets the world. A cluster of promises (Lauren Berlant). Xie expresses inconclusiveness with misfit gestures on the lawn, spasmodically. The recording chamber is the body. The body exudes this book of references and relations. Reaching out with love. Resist a preemptive staging (forward). Revelations come in reconnection. Afterward will have been a history, the names were etched long ago. Craze-raze epic naming at an amazing loss, this is a mass extinction (for everyone except the homo sapiens, yet). Swarming the body with meanings, writhing and writing through war: we are these wars we make with our dollar bodies. We give into these plateaus, then abrade the inner content. Xie haunts those trophy flowers, the ones with the gaseous rings. The irrepressible hangover of existential messages: KEEP CALM AND CARRY ON. Ask your bartender. all of them what devastates herr alae who cant stop to mark thir thumbs ta plug tha hole gushing fruitlessly everyfish whos manifest aspect dearregardless, whos manifest asp OIL GUSHING UNABATED (Julian T. Brolaski) Joy algae? Joy thee slippery algae, this allegory, this aleatoric musical refrain. This, then is what cells did muster.

HYPER ESSAY: FLAGRANCE

for David Brazil

The war on dissent.

Target switch with monkeys. A little button lights up: the revenge knob. The light isn't from this location, this essay; it shines in a retroactive location stored in the collective mind, its direct whereabouts is not easily locatable. And so it shines on. It goes without saying that state sanctioned violence has been the most virulent form of trauma imposed. A four-paneled screen. Painted on the screen: a palm tree, an Arab grave. (Jean Genet). Swat teams, heavy artillery, armed personnel carriers, bombs laced with spent uranium, tanks, thermal sightarmored reconnaissance airborne assault vehicles, anti-aircraft systems, artillery and mortars, humvees, self-propelled howitzers, multiple launch rocket systems, Apache and Chinook, assault amphibian vehicle personnel and air craft carriers...

We were standing on the steps of the New York Public Library literally anticipating Shock and Awe reigning down on Baghdad. Our bodies were stiff and edgy, an unrecognizable affective state shifted the somber mood, our friends accumulated. Nathaniel had a huge banner of *Guernica* which he painted in his tiny apartment. We rotated from side to side to hold the banner and read poems by Iraqi poets. Pedestrians offered wan smiles, shyly glanced in our direction, occasionally we were heckled. A suspended state of apprehension, on granite steps anticipating devastating violence as promised by our president. I felt nauseous. Unease as a national state of consciousness. When we ended our protest N and I had a slice of pizza and I bit into a plastic fork and accidently swallowed one of the prongs. Such a piece of crap fork to choke on. Morton's fork, Buridan's ass and *Tarzan of the Apes* depicted on a coffee cup. Obsolete before birth.

Between a donkey and an elephant. That bear, that bull. Peacocks strut the fantastic garden enclosure (nature as hyperreal and simulacral in an out of body sense) prior to the nuclear fallout reaching within the walls. Rockets are focused on this garden. Poetry appears that sure entrance to a storied paradisiacal garden, where pure patented mystique fulfills its indispensable acts your passion's kiss maintained against our age. (John Wieners) They try to foist on us the impression that they have eagle eyes. This was 2003. The protracted wars of our compromised futures—stability simply not lucrative to corporate enterprise—the deranged protocol of neoliberalism—we are construed to grin and bear it, link up with its needs. The physical recognition of our collective losses is a blowback governing the weather of the commons. The nucleated circle that we call a town square, what comprised of the commons—this was razed, then the ice broke up. The magnitude of each instance pronounces itself until we become proxy fighters for basic social services. Over the decade it is noticeable how protests have changed and the dynamics of the police have become more stringent and paralyzing. Kettling techniques and barricades introduced militarized structural realities as did instant holding cells and human nets. A common technique to dissuade marchers is to slow down mobility and quarantine bodies so that people feel cagy and paralyzed having to stand endlessly in place. Michael Elmgreen and Ingar Dragset created a number of sculptures they titled, "Powerless Structures". One such fabrication is situated outside the gallery space, submerged in the ground. The structure is a room without a ceiling—viewers peer into the space from ground level: loamy earth surrounds. It is a barren whitewashed room with a partition in the middle of an utterly anonymous, uninhabited space. There are two toilet paper dispensers on the wall—it is difficult to make out what these metal objects mounted on the wall are for. On one side of the partition there is a table and a chair. One thinks of rendition and interrogation centers, though one imagines them not to be so sterile and white. One imagines blood and stains, dirt and sweat clinging to the walls. The torturer wears an anonymous black hood while doing his job, shredder metal crashes through the cubical 24-7. The tools of confession are sharp. It is a bunker yet it is open to the elements. Marches upon marches. We committed to protesting on the steps of the New York Public Library every Thursday afternoon, Nathaniel and I. Gasps cloister/my armory, the crowds. (E. Tracy Grinnell) Critical mass protests happened frequently during the start of the second war on Iraq. Many of the marches after the initial mega marches at the start of the second war on Iraqi became as much about protesting Israel's expansion of settlements, the horror in Gaza and other pressure points in the Middle East. Elmgreen and Dragset's piece seems to refer to Brian O'Doherty's essay, "Inside the White Cube" (originally published in *Artforum* in 1976) which stated the rather obvious, all too often missing point: the gallery space is not a neutral container, but a historical construct—it is an aesthetic object containing (exuding value/generating value) in and of itself. Stuff into that supreme box all the institutional critique, social politics, performance and language and you still have a corporatized space that clamps down meaning. Empty it out as Elmgreen and Dragset have; meaning and content continue to arise from the vault. In the age of war, many trendy urban middle class dwellers choose to transform their living quarters into white rooms that resemble gallery cubes. Surveillance devices are set on their nannies and cleaning staff from discrete points in the ceilings, in furniture. It is totally teed up: nuclear arsenals now face Iran and other strategic locations. Some of them even wear pastel pants on the weekend with embroidered ducks, dogs and pheasants on them. False hope is a smothering devise of thick felt. Marching as coalition building and a show of solidarity—the rude camaraderie brought out by war; we yell out admonishments and call for change in a long column, hoarse and overwhelmed. Desire turns into contorted muscle memory of standing in line for hours on asphalt made of the oil from the oil fields, shouting into each other's protester ears, delineated from the merging crowds outside the barricades and police blockades; echo chambers, signs flashing around us. *Security and privatization, security and privatization.* The state is anxious about citizens storing weapons in their genitalia. *Systemic abrogation of rights, machines tallying up numbers.* Announcement #1: You can now be arrested if you protest in front of a federal agent even if it is impossible for you to recognize that there is a federal agent in your vicinity. Announcement #2: Monsanto's internal memos/computers were hacked by Wikileaks/Anonymous! NDAA and HR347: totalitarian democracy sham. Cognitive dissonance: the fox and the grapes. Cloned narcissist panic fascination. Cloaked endemic illness (anthropomorphized earth combines with transuranic waste effect). It would be sicker yet to resign our energies and acquiesce totally, don't you think. I begin to read the text scripted by The Invisible Committee, their tract called "The Coming Insurrection". I begin to read *After the Future* by Franco Bifo Berardi. One way to understand this mess is to see the state apparatus as a vampiric motif (or the zombie motif with slight modifications). The glowering vampire is the alter ego thriving on the fear and vitality of the body social, hustling us out, exposing us as individuals, breaking down communal sensation into tangible, internalized, personalized fear. The walking dead deliver an allegory for a condition that will be, very shortly our near future. The media is pimped by the state tantalizing narration with the blood of conquest, falsifying accounts with a prosody that proliferates bubbles. Summarizing and synthesizing, summarizing and synthesizing. We have to spend all this time reappropriating social connections, realizing again that our autonomy has become truly allergic to laws and recrimination. We have to reorganize on a continual basis. A thing need not be intelligent to be "alive," not alive to be intelligent, nor be either intelligent nor alive to reproduce itself. (Agnes Denes) Maybe something likewise is conveyed in your chapbook, *Mass of the Phoenix (A Mina Loy Portal)* by your passage: "It's all on the internet people! undead avatar" as dead and alive thoughts mingle in a steady, chunky stream of information and affect. A side note to this scenario of the wreckage of the dead and alive, Mario Galzigna via Silvia Federici, "…the epistemological revolution operated by anatomy in the 16th century is the birthplace of the mechanistic paradigm. It is the anatomical *coupure* that breaks the bond between microcosm and macrocosm, and posits the body both as a separate reality and a place of production, in Vesalius' words: a factory (*fabrica*)." The bourgeois subject (a body continuum) experiences this trouble all the time. When Calvin Klein Euphoria™ is sprayed on nubile bodies the mist sprays past the body contour into the universe. A school on Cape Cod had to shut down after there was an outbreak of respiratory issues caused by excessive use of body sprays by the teen school population. The body rebellion begins. Vapors bond with helium and hydrogen and cling to the gas dwarfs in the solar system. The new weapons they carry defy hand to hand combat. Civic space is retracted, the space for political expression is proscribed. We were not allowed to step foot on Wall Street! The entire street was cordoned off. Several blocks away Zuccotti Park was being occupied. Human flows on thoroughfares are highly contested. We pay taxes all of our lives and suddenly from one moment to the next, access is denied.

I should mention too, the gaudy effects that were used at this time to light the façade of the Stock Exchange. The building was illuminated by giant red floodlights. A tidal wave of cops (Victoria, Occupy Wall Street). Bloomberg's army. Symbolic violence tactically displayed throughout the park. The police came and knifed down the tents at the six month juncture of protest. Consternation and passion—what will these affects afford? We've seen submachine guns, they haven't yet been aimed. So far we haven't seen any combat dogs. We know they are being trained. Slight infractions presents the law in all of its violence. Cecily McMillian remarked on the radio today (after being in and out of hospitals and jails) that she gets through the difficulty of the world we live in by participating as an activist. She acquired a black and blue bruise in the shape of a hand on her chest from a police officer. We know about the BigDog™, born in the labs of MIT. BigDog™ is funded by the Defense Advanced Research Projects Agency (DARPA) in the hopes that it will serve as a robotic pack mule to accompany soldiers in terrain too rough for conventional vehicles. There is surely an urban application being planned as well. One OWS committee I briefly participated in before OWS dissolved was interested in originating a set of body positions that could be used to nonverbally communicate peaceful intentions. Adrenal channels stream the present, the now-ever, hyperpresent meeting the invisible walls of space—alive, molecular. Eyes tipped in vital space to handle representation. We are coming back again. We will envelop you (cops) (money) (power) (law). Quantum, limpid, othering: it. (Gracie Leavitt) Every practice brings a territory into existence—a dealing territory, or a hunting territory; a territory of child's play, of lovers, of a riot; a territory of farmers, ornithologists, or *flaneurs*. The rule is simple: the more territories there are superimposed on a given zone, the more circulation there is between them, the harder it will be for power to get a handle on them. (The Invisible Committee) To wear the bodysuit of rebellion from here on in. Power differences, inferiority, subjugation toys and ugly tendencies—we will be with you. A complex prison becomes the entire stage. *They days.* The advent of the Occupy movement in the United States has taken the time-honored discourse surrounding "the crisis of criticism" to a new level of intensity. One might even say it has brought the discourse surrounding the crisis of criticism into crisis, drawing out the etymological affinity between the words in question. As declared by the 16 Beaver Group for its nine-day convergence of artists, writers, and organizers from Egypt, Greece, Spain, Palestine/Israel, Chile, Oakland, Chicago, New York, and elsewhere this January: "The Crisis of Everything Everywhere." Respecting no boundaries, permitting no outside, this omni-crisis has severely destabilized the cultural and artistic fields in which criticism has traditionally found its home. (Talib Agápē Fuegoverde) The state is just a transplanted heart, prone. We become the totality of the environment we live in. The militarization of sense.

YOUR DOLLAR PROBLEM

How some Americans

olice want you only to

ioning. We love you, ca

SUBSISTENCE EQUIPMENT

Struggling city skeletal intermingle serial order existence
Inner in house enthralled blouses bodice   receptive
Envelops physical body tubs of water

Interpretive they appear gas lit engorged don't cause
Moving about distance over bridge turmoil
It is a big city bigger than any forest

When occurs light wood event
Scrutiny display as brilliant as I know
They show it

Leaves merge with paper
With soil grit shit glass
Step into truncation

Astonish
Swagger
Knowledge

It must be painful
Pushcart landscape mote circumference belief
Pursuit of exercise condition methodologically

Auditor measures ruler
In this refusal a grid developed
It must come out of you somehow as was said

•

Contained accumulation
Not really
Not really

Quiet
As a
Mirror

New blood
Rests on your
Delivery

Singular path
To
Cartoon protagonist

It is all the same with hay
Long way to the house animal full for a week I grieved tea in your place
Drove on somehow day without habitual science fiction

Straight lines
Rock crystals like amethyst
By the fence cured and coming

Now she smoothes off the rough edges with a file
They call it stealing off
I do to the moon

•

Deep country signified by fences terrain absolution
Virginity sheds waterfall likely and witches, blemishes
Slightest movements held together by glue

On a swing for fatality
Clean as the fall
One blame is love to chrome

Teething statement   I agreed shady
Sincerity holds ardor
Waves of energy in peregrinations

Physical mixtures, your proportion a valence atomic
Included molecular weight   constituents of mine
Show me open country   Bashō skin, skin

Trounced dunk in the marsh by estuary where Mohawk are
Instinct frames obligation
A ploy for collision

Silence is as abstract as you can get
Without a chart
Want is revamped

Spectrum from camp to candor
Webs generate an emotion that once was
Yours

•

My brain is chagrined
Because of this building material (now)
Watch how RNA counteracts DNA's determinations

Who do you go to of whom you've come from
Gravity hairy expansive desert
Sharks culminate saline abounds out of water

Annihilations index alienation
Robotic incision
Suspended over a precipice

Born in reflection glitch is dark
Tongues control buildings
The form of the occupant the form of experience

On a positive
Note notice exploitation
Zoology's sarcasm

And observation a woodpecker
Prophetic moon factory farm
Hermitage in a string of sweat

This edge represents paper
Dovetailed are the eyes
Morning, eastern standard time zone nebulae

•

Formalist islet   obdurate
Leading to? Your best guess and or how perception
Conceals war spoils insidious sidewalk weed cracked

Stray dog
The sneakers flung over the tree branch signify death
Indicate like a peony the dog the tree

Still life shattered when the helicopter
Flew by
Fires in windows never abated

Sling all hope with a measuring tape
Trope timbers tear looking upside down
Constituents where you vote

A tribal alphabet dances for Brecht
Newspaper consortiums snort lingo
Poets sidle by the bar the deciduous forest

We take to it nature
Lowdown fable
Entropy feature techno wasteland

Easy field set-up blinds
Get you into the action quicker
Accommodates mossy oak shadow grass

●

Conceals your dog
In low profile
There is a built-in floor

Not dark enough
Optically
Drink with the world

I could kill
You and eat
You with my Bowie knife

Verbal contest
For our ghetto
Concerns itself with itself

Separate events from time
And there is another planet
Realized in the solar system

The effected quality
Mistaken as future
Cowered at the flux

Isn't it finally time
We do away with the emphasis
On things

•

Our
Prosthetic
Other

Focus the vista
I cannot do that
Sir

I will not
Accuracy in
Small durations

Misleading quandary
Like straight lines
They nullified another

Back seat filled with enervate
Memory, passion steers outside
Chronology

The formation of this period
Has to do with angles and their vertexes
Dimensions find shape and cling

Axiomatic vat tannery where skins are
Lorded gutted to last gaunt mammal-less
Reptile bones explode into soap

●

Take this voluptuous gift
Of walking   seeming inevitabilities
Sentences   invisible light ray signals abreast

Seasons stray, migrate, south is south
In the northern zones
Mutual aid   piccolo rain

It rained on TV
Substantially—as in dearth, darth, dart, invasion
Herculean as in foot soldiers in a smoldering

Desert encrusted with casualty
Swashbuckling coal mine ore trove
Oil's slippery ilk

Steadfast in a bunk bed bunker with buddies
Caterpillar canary pond frog
Hogs from industry's tin forest

Falseness famish factoid pearl embellished
Emblematize roil murk the soil, exploitation
Before congressional vacations

You feel dismayed when I taunt political
Drenched in a tree's optic shade
Take my wrist and wrest it—pulsation

•

Instead of sex I wrote this
Efface lie lie there it was this sex
Our bed bulges with books shock shook music

My female friends are ambitious luscious ambitious
Wear bra and jeans while writing this
She said your life as if a fate on a swing boiling

Comparing modalities from a beehive
Chamber chamber quarter room domain house housed
Sip off this beaker sturdy proof hops choice silty liquidation

In the deciduous forest expanse was trimmed trimmed
Primed pools trickle ooze a tributary a mountain stream
Dash and claim the bodies commingle the bodies arch

Each time each line linear when supposition freedom
Elmer's Glue All shows bull maybe because glue is
Ground down hooves to paint my lips and speak to you

Hooves, and now I'd like to focus on
The aerial celestial view
Of the bathroom

As social rejection someone muttered
He sees spectrally
Oh my says my aunt grunt tree whiz

•

This gets better the product gets better
Thick pink slabs of pork and loads of butter
Opinionated, loaded, smart foolhardy and

Stereoscopic project facility
Hollyhock bolt the sky still holds vituperators
Martin Luther King Junior, the polis, haven or lawn

Sister is tuberous not morose monkey fingers
Promotion of vision civic duty, a documentary
To instill fright in the most steely taller bubbly

Make amends with insects because they watch our
Every move
I feed them and they need no clothing we reside

Who'd be foolish enough to give up
Loving women as a storm impales a gaze
This form will become norm predation ease

Relapse irk ooze substantiate
Delicate tower of flesh
Harvest diskette docket wild unsubstantiated desire

To be
Shall we want to fuck
Kindly move these Christmas cacti

•

Aficionado of fire water
Nobody still knew
Artichoke

Sorta medicinal not green herbs
Not to explain excellence vermouth disgust
Jim Jones ritual sports nation small or medium

To swim in rookie girl's colors like pink
I don't even care in the souvenir store
Military fatigues red socks and underwear

At the real place 96 degrees hot day to do this
So political so integrated woo you over
Can't complain instead of job every night

Every night to be discovered by the Western world
To be murdered try to read too much of the leaflet
Dreaming of the night when I can sit down and read

You said sherry what I meant to say
So wound up just a person single person a little bit alone
Coming off of it new a lot of fun

Summarized into a pit
Telephone conversation itemization of day's forlorn
Enterprise surmised by sisters

•

It might be too much to ask of the economy
Without light as we service heat this is an iron mine
The mountain top was decapitated

Morgue standards for temperature by your sofa a prime
Number doesn't get hot! Certainly not when football hurls
Insults when TV shows synonymous with Fallujah crosswalk

Don't wake up or do when break up can't get water
And the streets clamor there is fire
Everywhere my son is on fire

Dusk rover nightfall he wakes we collaborate
Edicts documents bills a refrigerator with organic
Merchandise

Helicopters survey our hood about the tree line
The dissidence has cicadas hush in a season of mating
Terrorism is on the rise it is a brutal field suddenly

A statement is antithetical to reason and into a slammer
Stammer ritual courting warden section something
Guaranteed rights freed this is the law make amends

Treason burden burgeon and operatively to be sublime
Come on now move over vote stance gut
The cross is hard made of hard wood there is hardly

•

Any remaining in the forest
Microphone twang and dic•tion•ar•y
Anarchistic tick timber resource, sit here the jungle

Crocheted
In camouflage
Colors

Someone says
In the
Background

Faces
Wear out
Fastest

Philosophies
Of sex
And eating

Popcorn
Carrots, for
Dinner

Crop circles
Pathogens
Gene pool's stewardships

•

Trouncing a truncated trunk
As in an adage
Articulates wattage

Rancor smokes swords lingually
Poem ions became are ore brewed and belted
As if fantasies were stationary

Back hoe alloy
Archaeology— dug up behind you
A culture buried in snow

Images trigger registers
Heart monitors blinking intensively caring
Throb oft blaring read red sequences

Vote gate bubble gait
Run till there's no world around
A hemisphere's anguish satellite dish

Terror as an extremity of reason
no-holds-barred bifurcated by legislation
Permeable as jewelry carbon as a base

Either poached a rock or source
Sheen of fashion waxen
Puckered squelched envelopes speak petition

•

Stone maven
Innuendo forlorn
In a rock

Fantasy enthraller interlocutor
Play is precarious
Hallucinatory phenomena taxiing

Congealed belief produces tracts
Purring feathers
Stress their outpourings

Filaments and vellum
Buckle down bellwether
Tangible object/relic

Familiar thing
Or else
Heads up to the sky

I see flames, etc.
To the hands come
Many suggestions

Has this
Crystallized
Into a mass

•

Obliterates etchings
Jet sprayed, gaze
Too costly for repairs

Stray dog
Topography
Folkloric for a theme of street

Declines its time
Brisk velocity
Infinitive swarm

By the cathedral cold water
By the cathedral a vat of cold water
Bottled water by the cathedral

Traversal
Trapeze
That

Placed sized priced
Identity fields of maize
Grow on until traversal

Exclamation
Tin horn bull horn whistle
A sounds alarms bombs indenting implosive

•

Encased in gravity glass gall description
Pen's ink alcohol tobacco firearm
Incense burns at the temple

Hard to relinquish each claim claimant
Substantiated by blood and image
The particulate matter what is held accountable

Stuff a down pillow with My Lai
Sawed off
Spent uranium

It's all there
As soil in sharp contrast
Stomach, in the stomach public

Winter soldiers
Call dire
Documentary horror

A utensil for council
To cut with to fork with
To spoon spool spoil

Care   :   cargo
Crewmembers   :   cargo
Durable goods   :   care

•

Odalisques Siberian Croatian Laotian
American career girl cleavage
Convince the law where commodities end

Tirade moniker
Immersion bane
Ratcheted up to strangest denominator

Gristly self-perpetuating doom
Slinks along the lawn
Couched in sizes

Outfit joy with your third hand
Eye. To. Eye.
Such a session with immersion

By every account
Compendium Neanderthal
Watch for arctic ash and other whiteness

Penal comprehension
Of time
And space

Money, Mississippi
Whistle this
Genocide

●

This effigy of dust
Biographical skin
Scattered to the winds

Tally ho leeward below the kneeling
Involutedly lines of a gesture partake
Cerberus. Souls sited, resistance deep

Nocturne as the web is spun
Windows let a simple breeze through
Demarcation comes where frame seals

Summer perches on the crest of tree
The parchment and the parched convene
Dogs urinate on the hedges graffiti buttresses

Presently printed books decorate librarians
Svelte is soon to be in print
Ink preens, attention

The significance of scissors sidles alongside
Book spines
Thin and sublime overhead ruined chapel

Congratulations fugue registered as D sharp
As if the manuscript meddled
Sunglasses reassure the delicate optics of spark

•

A spiral jetty extends out from a dead lake
A chance you take is in screening
Wite-out works well for typographical mistakes

Rancor wrestles with the calculator
A heritage genetic to brawl
Pens take on penmanship

Pressure per second as the hands go round
Chain reaction. Fire just can't
Melt steel, trust trusses hell bent lattices

The picture defies physics
Hydrocarbon effects compared to the impact
Of RDX

A supersonic blast detests
Smithereens breeze pulverized concrete
Put aluminum to flame

Structural engineers' lips sealed
Directs attentions with flailing arms
Ammunition, manumission same for regime

Papal yoke green back chattel
Monetize the last last node
Willage

•

Sinister' commemoration
Black roses balk vases
Encased by vulcanization

Huge
Red
Tide

Running
Running
Waters

What of
Deters
Her

Avers
Oars
Levers

Coronet
Croons
Crests

Stratosphere
Sheer
Awareness

•

Gave
Vat
Gave

Mouth
Soaring
Mouth

For how
It might
Have happened

Bore in equilibrium
Elucidation brain floats
A cranium

Wedgwood cinderblock headwork
In profile its fat private
Mediumistic substance exchanged for ink's oil

Voices of water
Disturb
Delirium

Fugue gold
Wedged by viscous
Wetness

•

Before
Buildings
Were felled

Icon implosion in a perfect storm
A flag was painted to mimic thread
Mimic wind mimic paint imploded

Paintbrush from the hair of her plume
Poem written with the hair of bear
Hair of fox hair edict in rabbit

Gunned down trophy wolf of deer
Rabbits in the thicket
Hiding out in sleep

Farce turned upside down is read
The point of the matter inverted
What felt through cracks is want

Sharpen pencils with kitchen utensils
Acrobatic knives
Miniscule edges glisten expression

Candelabra held up to abjection
Where nothing was there
Nothing was there in its depiction

•

Invent equity
Intervention vector
Vexation factor

Mood equity lyric under 10 watt light
What is withheld shimmers in a chalice
To your lips each drop exceeds flavor

By the canyon we walk hand in hand
This is a local phenomenon
Buildings create a valley

Atmospheres present their staging
Rust vets water
Screams in the night beneath the tree

Initiate prowess
There are echoes
And replays

High register vocable
Decibels scratch
More variant than horror

She hurls herself at him
I look on lying in bed
He folds over onto brick

•

When eyes
Leopards
Are

This causes water
Down's loftiness is soaked
Saline expunged

The body's a prop (if)
What then
Of each utterance

The musical layer
Fabric draped around legs
Windows regain solidity

Inner chamber relegated by sound
Choked of information
It is possible to hydroplane

The queued up order
Is intercepted
By some terminology, a harbinger

Suddenly the technology
Won't support
Thought

●

Space has
No
Patience

Cotton with its thorns, railroad ties, Napa Valley crops

    Then water came

Who is to blame
Maim abandon seepage rot
Naught
Aught
I'd

Say
I'd

Consolidate
Feelings with this lot
History that presses
Live sensations
Whatnot
Not what
Life functions
Crudity
Incredulity

It was on this day in ——that

HYPER ESSAY: BOTCHED ESSAY ON SYMTOMATIC VIOLENCE IN THE USA

for Cecily McMillian and Marie Mason

Cataclysm mocking with 12 tipping points cartooned on the bulletin board for a Googled planet under pressure. High register vocables report grim impressions, babies born without limbs in semi-cordoned off nuclear zones abandoned decades after conflagrations. In medical test sites where participants realize too late the injection was meant for experiment not healing. The graphics depict West Antarctic ice shelves tearing apart. Amplification days. These are threshold days. If we take into account these drastic shifts in the meaning of "violence," a much less self-evident point emerges—that violence is a *discursive* rather than an *ontological* category. Even some of the most astute political thinkers and philosophers who have written extensively on the question of violence have treacherously presumed, or even argued for, the ontological nature of violence. But if we take violence as a *discursive construct,* we can see how it has become a crucial terrain upon which the state wages a war against political dissent. Currently, it is being pushed to the limits of the intelligible in order to accommodate the expanding authority of the state to prosecute and eliminate different forms of political resistance against deepening austerity. (Anonymous contributor, "On Violence and Non-Violence, Once Again: Lessons from Recent Political Developments on the Berkeley Campus", Part 1) I've been totally engrossed in all the postings relating to violence on our listserv. My own hesitance to comment on and pinpoint symptoms relating to the black box phenomena has to do with the fact that violence is so multivalent, prevalent and systemic and it replicates itself into new formations so constantly/consistently that I find it nearly impossible to synthesize my thoughts. It doesn't make sense to isolate considerations of black box techniques used at several demonstrations from the steady state of violence condoned by our imperial core.

A pledge to nonviolent struggle seems deceptively pure and unreal. Struggle suggests violence. Us with no you or I (Ed Roberson). Laws we have only partially arrived at consensually carry out sublime, ideological violence cloaked as protection. We are subject to these laws. A majority tacitly accepts these laws. Laws do the job of prepping society for specific outcomes. How else could it be that 1.46 million African-American men out of a total voting population of 10.4 million have lost their right to vote? Or that Native Americans have ended up on the crappiest land and have to constantly scramble to negotiate any semblance of "rights" for their nations with the US government acting as supreme judicial force, or that women's wages are dramatically less than men's, or that women have to remain hyper vigilant of their own body agency? If you ask me, living an American lifestyle of any sort is a form of violence. Trained to be a teddy bear and a killer. (Douglas A. Wissing) On this note, how many teddy bears have ended up in landfills and won't they all end up there? Afflictions. According to the Western psyche human worth is summoned through conflict, through the clashing of fragments across the ozone. History then accrues as the perfect cholera of density, so that its necessity transpires through heaps of counted bodies which configures in the rational mind as honed embryos in the system. (Will Alexander) How we procure our foods, how we get to work, what our work consists of, how we relate to the environment, how we educate kids in toxic laden schools, how we cope with aging, how we take care of our bodies, how we dump our waste, how we relate to each other, etc. We find ourselves ever-presently in a theater of war. Prescription drugs are the number one killer in this country. Vicious circles form around a massive death wish whirlpool sucking device of motorized technology so that all fields are killing fields. For two days I found myself passing the 30 foot tall Victoria's Secret™ models depicted on herculean banners attached to a corner building at 34ᵗʰ Street. Each day I tried to meet their gaze, it was impossible—their pupils stare out 5 floors up. Their nearly nude sculpted bodies made a flagrant statement about flesh memory. Their bodily postures refuse identification, they've been instructed to perform sexual availability and untouchability in an airbrushed blend. Their massive forms defy sensuality; the scale and context transcend corporality. I wanted to find something human about their presence and then I realized this ad campaign defies what it means to be human. A Sphinx-like and entropic projection dissipating with the fashion season, a cynical finality, a conception that the signifiers suffer. These women aren't prostitutes for capitalism; they are a reflecting mirror of the capitalist imagination. They announce bloated becoming. None of the affective cues of challenging contemporized life (where histories crowd all presences into forward motion) affect them: that's why they can be shown wearing negligees on a cold spring day, their bodies larger than any sauroposeiden or brontosaurus, larger than any mammal that has ever roamed the earth—if paleontological data is accurate. I want to connect, find a way to empathize with their condition, instead the feeling is puzzlement from one day to the next. I feel like I should return again and examine my relation to this space and press to realize what these women are doing there. They are not enigmatic, they are not mysterious, they don't have an aura, and they do not create tension: they are like a void, like a negative space in a continuum. I assure you then, that I know a limp and clammy handshake when I shake one and I will say hello and I will treat you like a human but I wonder, will you do the same? (Lindsey Boldt) Treat you like a human: that's such a complex function. Humans constantly override what it means to be animal and insist on exemplary and exceptional status, it has led here, to alienated apartheidism or something more menacing (than division) because if we humans want something we are fine displacing whatever previously thrived here. The surface tension of violence is deceiving. The US cultural paradigm focuses on symptomatic violence and covers up core systemic violence. I can't get my mind off of James Lee who took people hostage at the *Discovery Channel's* headquarters in September, 2010 and was subsequently shot and killed by police. The media instantly dispatched a characterization of Lee as completely demented and shut down any meaningful discussion that might have arose from his actions and plangent message about animals. It is too easy to ridicule and exploit the desperation at the base of Lee's gestures. Protesting is often read as extreme, hysterical and excessive. Emotions have become medicalized diagnostic tools for an industry attempting to achieve one unified placid social body so saturated by chemicals that functioning outside of the system becomes improbable. There's little candor, disclosure or transparency around violence. Secret extraordinary rendition. People waited patiently in line, hoping to be fucked suddenly, either under a painting or, if possible, inside the painting, where the colors would swathe, coil, and transfigure, such as in the benevolent psychosis of infancy. (Miranda Mellis) A rude statistic: 25% of children have been diagnosed with mental illness in the United States. Society's relationship to "the sacrifice" is morphing rapidly. Needs of food, shelter, space at the base level all engender some level of violence. Incidental kills. This was a logging road. During colonial times all the trees on these hills were razed. The stumps were shipped to England to become vessels that sailed to Africa and other continents. The stumps became furniture, weaponry and fuel (whale fat could only illuminate a portion). Because you still listen, because in times like these to have you listen at all, it's necessary to talk about trees. (Adrienne Rich) Yes. Yes, I saw Earth's Seventh Circle come down. A door is half-opened on the courtyard. Two policemen carry a person alive/dead. I see the handcuffs the paleness and mostly the catatonic state of the body. (Etel Adnan)

HYPER ESSAY: WHAT IS THE DIFFERENCE IN MEANING BETWEEN "AND" AND "OR"?

for HR Hegnauer, who posed this question

And tends to conjoin, adds to a preexisting condition, there's excess built into the population of this word, and tension, as when adding extras, come lately. Or is hesitant and coveys judgment predicated on the way balance teeters. Exclusionary. Objects separable. Paradise and Armageddon. Armageddon or paradise. Crowded underpinnings could be disrupted or remain sedentary. Crowds trample, also crowds indicate mass movement and general consensus, and change is ushered in with crowds. There are joyful crowds. Mostly it is my impression that crowds come together out of mutual agitation and need. Crowds are radicalized individual bodies acting out their merging solidarities in concert. The men and women in the crowd argued with her and one another. They kept crossing the road, and some came inside the wall. Yet they did more or less clear the way. If the foreman had no experience in bossing a mob, they had no experience in being one. Members of a community, not elements of a collectivity, they were not moved by mass feelings there were as many emotions there as there were people. And they did not expect commands to be arbitrary, so they had no practice in disobeying them. (Ursula K. Le Guin) Usually and is the more responsive term. At a juncture, an ultimatum, a barrier to more ands. Possibilities for the body: and is the operative condition for change that holistically reflects agency and presence. And allows proliferation and open-endedness. And furnishes an escape route out of dogmatic categorization and compartmentalizing—my body for one is and. Or doesn't extend, there's no room for the ethereal, gross and sublime body extensions that grasp beyond the fleshy outline we call self. These outer realms are necessary to inform the self which seemingly exists within a contour. Or tends to sponsor false distinction or naturalized difference. There is a latent hesitancy in regards to or. Or others possibility, something else comes into play, recharges, disturbs or fortifies. And: historical accumulation. Or: choice, will, listing. Polarizations. A way to compel the details and subtleties of a philosophical inquiry: and. Pyramidal versus circulation. And: combinatory, or: extinction or extermination. Tears in the eyes and a thick feeling in the throat. Ummm,   , killer killeth, or fixated attention on <u>or</u>. Anthony Perkins turns his head in five incremental movements rather than one continuous motion. It was like bricks in a wall, clearly countable, not like the flight of an arrow or a bird. (Don DeLillo) Rather is or's dependent cousin, so much more elegant, under the radar and acting as a device to slice out action, reposition the camera, refocus the iris to the less obvious projection. Rather is firmly attached to the next possibility in the sequence that is already forecasted, anticipating an intervention from the discerning being attending to action. Rather is imbued with cultural expectation and its variations. The words themselves find formation as in a marching band chiming in when there is lyrical necessity, taking cues from semiotic rules operating outside of cognition. Here a direction the land drowned or revealed or ex-posed (Larry Eigner) A shift in delicacy and a verbal refusal of the tyranny that or supports on occasion. I would prefer not to (Herman Melville), I would rather not… Often following rather is the word than, so watch how action functions: Politically it is never a particularly good idea to first tell people that they are your equals, and then humiliate and degrade them. This is presumably why peasant insurrections, from Chiapas to Japan, have so regularly aimed to wipe out debts, rather than focus on more structural issues like the caste system, or even slavery. (David Graeber) A two-place logical operator says to another, "Habeas Corpus has been eliminated". But wait, I say, my name is May I have my body back! It doesn't matter; this edict came down as an executive order that was passed at a minute before the New Year. Conjunction-junction, what's your function. Idempotency, monopotency, truth-preserving, false presencing, commutativity, associativity and distributivity to say the least. Our fallacy forum is filled up; no one additionally will be admitted. Good luck! The killer's name is imprinted on everyone's memory: Norman Bates, but nobody remembers the victim's name. Anthony Perkins is Norman Bates, Janet Leigh is Janet Leigh. The victim is required to share the name of the actress who plays her. It is Janet Leigh who enters the remote motel owned by Norman Bates. (Don DeLillo) Don DeLillo's character, the former military mastermind understands this conversion (back) into stones. Say it with stones!

I postponed this essay until the last—with only four days to go and near a closing point (intent on writing 10,000 words between March 1st, 2012 and April 1st, 2012 to supplement the poems in *Early Linoleum* with a form of writing that disturbs their gravitational presence—the hyper essays). The writing of the poems in *Early Linoleum* spans a decade—slightly more than a decade actually, preliminary notations preceded September 11th, 2001. This body of work chronicles the disturbances of empire—the fallout its disasters precipitated and the spectrum of volatile states of consciousness that accompany a study of what it means to live within the dictated confines of a prison industrial military complex facing climate change, a toxified environment and the myriad challenges to animal. An explicit animal urge to choreograph and document words (biorhythms and sensations) related to pressurized meanings, the physical torsion that incubates within inscription, acculturated in our habitat: a habitus. And too, the need to gain access to the proliferation of encrypted meanings and insinuations, keying into the evasive and temporarily occluded, and then participating in that density with explosive steganography: hiding data in other data, camouflaging, blending and cohabitating in the vegetative understory; dynamics of the social running naked through the underbrush of divergent information. Missing referents, always the missing referents buried as they are, out of sight, wedged precariously, throbbing, and tangible, however postponed. For example, how distortions occur when animal is translated into human, or when gender is proscriptive. Geologic understandings guided the structural formation of these poems. A psycho-geological impetus hardwired soundings; material communicative vectors. Affective and somatic (volatile sensation, emotion) registers turned up, dubbed, and then overdubbed *a cacophonous vocalization*. An occasion to swoon by the trio of plastic swan planters filled with magenta colored impatiens while a pickup truck idled; such interstices. Then to recognize the retrieval process that is required to again open up an image at a post-experiential stage. Here we are, exercising the right to feel, negotiating spatial tenses where presence has been subtracted, where presence has been deployed and representation looms large casting shadowless aggravations. Mentality and the surround of interlocking motile structures. Language takes active body readings, monitors the internal and external situation and calibrates on-going communication. The poems undress sublimations and subcutaneous themes, and also excessive material, the viscera of performing darkness. At the core, defiance—there's this available spectrum that trumpets on the one hand bravado and on the other, a coy recklessness fastening in on abjection. All other lines of inquiry would be like walking backwards. You'll never see where you're going. You must begin with directors, assistant directors, adult authority boards, roving boards, supervisors, wardens, captains, and guards. (George Jackson) Concerned that these poems might become pillars or edifices (aestheticized to the point of stultification) (evacuation/excavation) I felt a spasmodic interactive need to inform on and with their tectonics, to dig through the rubble *the fallout of an unraveled social*: the aftereffects, the blinding sheen and terseness of social violence; the overwhelming abundance of state sanctioned industrial and technological violence normalized into law. Low rumbles, moans, clotting at the dig, reflection chains clangs. Deliberate and or stochastic particles. A study of how fat quarantines toxicity in the body. When parsing out an autonomy that atomizes and regroups in the atmosphere of the proliferating double bind of capital (and what it makes us do unbeknownst to ourselves)—to remark on these continual shocks of reckoning within the organs, blood and muscles of the personalized body indicating as a presence through reading and other mutual exchanges, actions and expressions. Mutations, changes, hesitations and torquing the angle of reach: forensics for the undead, exuberance notwithstanding the strife. Dying as a process is representational of living as a process. There is no statute of limitations when it comes to amelioration and remediation *inadequate words, some hear redemption*. Research movement vocabularies of the gestures that ameliorate suffering *this pose represents nonviolence, an offering*, etc. Is it possible to quarantine the effects of capital the way the body quarantines toxins that enter it? Or disambiguate in the face of capital, make ourselves illegible like foliage, exist in a way that capital can't comprehend because there is no bottom line involved. It is surely true that care is mutual aid. Gestures substantiate autonomies beyond friendship. Drain piousness, here, now. Rough and ready, thickly smeared. I tremble in doubt, divided by multiple entry points and explosive content wrapped in rambling overlays sent to the council on commentary, and without exception the animation either frenetic or dull, shifts to no options left, recognizing useless hope in the face of bomb holes caused by numbering digits. (kari edwards) Spasmodic body reactivity, quantum leaps; we find ourselves dredging the pool of Narcissus with our pantyhose and hugging moist larval shaped mummies of bloodied bandages, life sized, soft, improperly disposed of. In accident time where there are no accidents. You have no choice the choice comes after. (Sarah Kane) The decade bubbled up troupes and modalities of *de-living,* time closed in upon itself while giving the illusion that it was speeding into some future alterity without vantage point, deployed to mock history and any passage *into*: torture and detention, eradication of Habeas Corpus, identity politics morphed into post-identity bare life and personality sculpting (Martha Wilson), simulacra and liminality, war and prisons as economic backbone, genocide, dollar signs, the bling of personal consumption, cynicism—the democracy app is not working. (Van Jones) post-traumatic stress disorder, border guarding, security contractors, Gulf War Syndrome, the body as aftereffect (zombies, vampires, disposable peoples, refugees, the homeless, temporary workers, and general obsolescence) shrouded apprehension and embedded medias (or what's called *distanciated impression management* as coined by Sarah Maltby), disaster tourism, theme parks, domestication and procreation. The comfy home motif really took off after 911 (Controlled demolition anyone? 90,000 tones of concrete, metal, bodies and office equipment pulverized) and crashed during the housing foreclosure disaster in 2008—see Martha Rossler's photo collages for suggestive imagery) speculative finance, the blatantly faked ponzi schemes, software, hardware, archives, ALEC, dichotomies, "reliability" and other marketing phrases, the wholesale of the remaining commons, the administration of bodies, terrorism as pin the tail on the donkey not of the state or corporation but on the messenger, global climate change wrestling evolution doubters

(2,000 record breaking climatic events in the last month), mass extinction of animals, emptied out post-conceptualist conceptualisms, recycled by-products, unknown inorganic chemical mixes in waterways, islands of plastic, fracking and horizontal drilling, nuclear proliferation, mad cow syndrome, ebola, bird flu, expiration dates and shelf lives, executive orders, bailout bonus culture, Fresh Direct, school shootings, pathologized populations, genetic modification, reality TV, stateside militarisms and Code Orange lockdown of civil liberties, profiling, digital porosity, twitter rushes of techno electrical surges, exceeding and superseding, social performances of well-being, medical pharmacopeias, apocalypse narratives, yoga and third wave feminism is an incomplete, pockmarked list *myriad circumstances of capitalism's rationalizations of social reproduction*. Very particularly the ideas around difference were strung out and chewed through until a bleak market homogenization attempted to coat everything in industrial grade ideological Kevlar and now we gnaw through its restraint. An attempt at saying collapses into disarticulation, the intake moment is manipulated by global positioning. Our bodies are here, and here: episodic, traversing, reprogrammed, mental and physical *as we escalate out of politics* which could be signified by rescinding power dynamics that operate out of use value, disobeying the drill. Perforating the logistics of sensation is this mega syndrome of capital way beyond death—capital thrives on death. The jumpstart that death offers capital *executive order thematic*. We initiate crucial performances to find fissure within stealthy ideologies, ideologies we formerly could not name. The base or basis: decoding the episteme, signs and signifiers: the doxa. *We love for this fissure we fuck for this fissure.* Faulty repetitions, repetitions that reveal fault lines precisely where contradictions crack—let's aim to touch the voids with great caresses...We narrow in on symptomology and effect, a delayed reactive, somatic admission as we draw in closer. In the 1970's, films of Harry Houdini's escape techniques and magic were a popular distraction. Especially his mirror handcuff trick. A group of us teens watched avidly in the red velvet walled theater, once called *The Richmond* during the days of vaudeville shows, during our youth it was renamed *The Mohawk Theater* as it fell into disrepair along with the town. Desire, poised as if to escape a double bind. If I remember correctly, there was a trailer of Houdini that played before *Halloween* was shown one night in 1978. There was a kernel of something profound in juxtaposing

Houdini's getaway elegance alongside demented and angry Michael Myers performing his slashings in small town America, underscored by the fact that Houdini died on Halloween. An allegory for our hill town populous. The opening text is a prologue called "The Future Anterior". 'Glossematics, Thus' is an imaginary three-way conversation with/between/on Jacques Derrida, Tyrone Williams and Brenda Iijima quilted within autobiography, saturated by layers of socio-historical detail—sedimentary. Recessive archaic memory banks are water tables equalizing social pressures. 'Early Linoleum' involves ornate, opaque, highly aestheticized diction—a crystallization of social registers—tectonic shifts. 'Subsistence Equipment' is volatile, contentious, brash—igneous. I was thinking of the charged spaces within and between human structures, especially during states of perpetual strife, as in war—the dissonance, air, wind flow, coagulated ideas, anger—how frequencies diffuse or mutate—metamorphic—streaming from urban zones to country/wild—the blending of real and unreal distinctions. Stimuli agitated and amalgamated in living tissue—this is a corporeal report. Responses and responders entered the pool of affects, engendered distinct modes of being and presencing that were communally and personally experienced—these cues converted into language, a cognitive-physical effect, *prosody countering the economics of fungibles*. The phonemes mashed and bunched tighter together— words as compressed social deliberation (or delirium). Speech, thinking and writing are the anatomical mechanisms we use for meshing (creating a circulatory system). The mesh delivers feedback—exciting communication. Meanings expand—the contemporaneous moment always reaches forward and backward in time simultaneously—time, extralingual dimensionality. Previously polluted pasts melt with eventuated futures, what will have been stares at us elusively or dead-on in particularized, atomized light. Time recycles time and space *until it doesn't quite*. Mediated, unmediated, absorbing, absorbed: futures that bud in a garden of blooming tenses. Flowers of rad. (Sampson Starkweather) Could it be surmised that nature will have already been culture when we cathect our animality? The profane fecundity of everyness would absorb the holy. The holy would *already then* be extraneous. *Profane everyness gives*. Diaphanous, fibrous, vaporous, bone hard density meets epidermal softness as meaning moves through and emanates from membranes. My arms and legs dissolve in all directions. (Kim Hyesoon) Rotting breakdown is vitality, but what about the infrastructure, will it return as commons? It was a question of release. Having to solve a problem, especially a problem related to a confinement, was an immediate relief to me. I breathed easier being forced to breathe in order to move, in order to solve a problem, especially a problem related to the confinement of another person...(Inger Christensen) *You know, the restraining order forever held against unsanctioned histories.* Poems are social reality, all communicative behavior is, therefore the meanings generated are a living infrastructure suctioning onto surrounding existence as contortions and transitions occur. Thinking finds form in poems, poems act as recording devices, holding cells for substances; poems are black boxes (black blocs too—since bodies in blocs are what generate the force of movement as do syllables generated out of the body's mobility).

"The owl flies in the moonlight, over a field where the wounded cry out." Georges Bataille, trans. by Robert Hurley. *The Impossible* (San Francisco, City Light Books, 1991), 27.

All italicized words in "Glossematics, Thus" except the quotation from M. NourbeSe Philip are from Jacques Derrida, *Of Grammatology*, trans. Gayatri Chakravorty Spivak (Baltimore and London, The Johns Hopkins University Press). I've made slight modifications to the punctuation.

"Deter and mine me." Quotation from M. NourbeSe Philip, in conversation.

White man's foot print (or the plantain) is a common herb/weed that grows in lawns and in sidewalk cracks. It is edible and contains a lot of fiber. It was one of the nine sacred herbs mentioned in *The Lacnunga*, the most ancient source of Anglo-Saxon medicine where it was called "the mother of herbs." In old world tradition, plantains were used as a remedy for bleeding, cuts, burns, poison ivy, snake bites and inflammations, and a tea made from the seeds was employed to remedy diarrhea, dysentery, and bleeding from mucous membranes. Its spread has been thought to follow in the footsteps of the early colonists and their settlements across the continent. A report from Virginia, in 1687, stated that the Native American Indians called the plant "Englishman's Foot," due to the plant's habit of growing wherever the white man created a settlement, giving the plant two of its common names. See: http://www.herbalextractsplus.com/plantain.cfm

The King's Two Bodies refers to a book written by medievalist Ernst Kantorowicz, in which the issue of sovereignty is discussed. See http://plato.stanford.edu/entries/sovereignty/

Information about camphor is from Wikipedia.

"The forest is haunted by the specter of communism." Peter Linebaugh, *The Magna Carta Manifesto* (Berkeley and Los Angeles: University of California Press, 2008), 156.

"Now comes the flood and the obscuring of its source." Carla Harryman, *Adorno's Noise* (Ithaca: Essay Press, 2008), 9.

The word-concept "exergue" would require elaborate explication to reveal its multivalent and complex array of meanings. Derrida uses this word in rich variant ways. *Early Linoleum* interacts with Derrida's generative impulses.

"Mogorva" translates as morose in Hungarian; "drungalegur" translates as morose in Icelandic, "posępny" translates as morose in Polish. I'll purposefully leave the other non-English words untranslated in order to signal the *outside* that English often ignores or refuses to negotiate.

Most of the geological site-specific information refers to North Adams, Massachusetts—birthplace of the author.

Images in the cover and frontispiece collage, *Our Evocative Futures* (2004), are from the following:

"How the Air Was Created. The Anatomy of the Air": no artist accredited.

"The Undulating Atmosphere": no artist accredited.

"An Eclipse of the Sun": Mel Tinklenberg, for Buckbee Mears Company.

Painting, "Reptiles Inherit the Earth," *The Pageant of Life*. Courtesy of the Peabody Museum, Yale University.

Life Magazine, November 3, 1967: Runaway kids, advertisement for 1968 Chevy II Nova.

Life Magazine, September 11, 1970:

"At a June 19 rally in Los Angeles, Jane Fonda (right) made the financial plea for the Soledad Brothers legal fund and Angela Davis delivered a critique of criminal justice."

"Hello world." Ford Pinto car advertisement.

"The Aging Legion faces a new enemy." Image of a flag going up in flames at a rally of the People's Army Jamboree.

Life Magazine, November 1970: "This car's got more than corduroy buckets seats . . . "

Repeating Mickey Mouse image.

Money Image.

"Turn off this noisy world, Turn on a Ford," Ford advertisement.

Life Magazine, December 1979:

"Now you can wear your very own miracle." Casio watch advertisement.

"In 1976 white students from South Boston demonstrated against busing." Photo, Stanley Forman, *Boston Herald American*.

"In 1971, outside Orlando, Fla., Walt Disney World prepared to open its gates for business. When the last turret had been tacked in place on Cinderella Castle, all the denizens of the Magic Kingdom assembled for a grand ceremonial portrait with royal Mouseketeers Mickey and Minnie front and center." Photo, Yale Joel.

"Phan Thi Kim Phuc tore off her flaming clothes after she and other villagers were mistakenly napalmed by a South Vietnamese warplane." Photo, Huynh Cong Ut—AP—World Press Photo.

"Inmates showed solidarity with clenched fists during the 1971 rebellion at Attica prison in upstate New York."

"Tan Son Nhut air base was under rocket and artillery fire and looters were rampaging throught the city before Marine helicopters began landing on tennis courts and the tops of downtown buildings to lift a rear guard of 1,373 U.S. citizens away to ships of the Seventh Fleet."

"Near a flaring oil well in the Saudi Arabian desert a worker kneels toward Mecca to pray." Photo Marc Riboud—Magnum.

"Donna Summer became the undisputed Queen of Disco in '75 with her sizzling 'Love to Love You Baby.' Photo, Harold Smith.

"Bruce, a 25-foot polyurethane shark, played the heavy in *Jaws* and found it a part he could really sink his three rows of teeth into."

"In 1975 Patty Hearst left the San Maeo, Calif., jail for court. Sentenced to seven years for bank robbery, Hearst—kidnapped and 'brainwashed' by the SLA—was freed after serving 22 1/2 months."

"Tinkering with the very sparks of life, genetic engineering began to produce organisms unplanned by nature."

"The decade began with the biggest women's protest marches since the days of the suffragettes, 'I am a Woman.'"

Centerfold crotches all featured in *Life Magazine*, September 11, 1970, except C-3PO Marlboro Man.

Black Panthers, photo, Roger Bockrath.

Mikhail Baryshnikov, photo, Max Waldman.

John Travolta, photo, Douglas Kirkland.

Mark Spitz, photo, Stern—Black Star.

Cheryl Tiegs, photo, Walter Iooss—*Sports Illustrated*.

C-3PO, *Life Magazine*, December 1979.

Peter Frampton.

Evel Knievel, in centerfold (reverse).

Dickies model.

The additional collages that appear within this book were constructed using various *Life Magazine* issues spanning 1967–1980. All collages by Brenda Iijima, 2014.

ACKNOWLEDGMENTS

Thanks to Toshi for his living ideas of space, time, and love.

This thinking and writing is engulfed by the thinking and writing of so many co-genitors, some of whom are noted within the texts, others inferred. There is an abundance of sensitivity, care, and joy experienced among other presences as we absorb and thrive on the nutrition of dispersed offerings. I've marked many of these unions in the text—dialogues of reciprocity, simultaneities of togetherness, and autonomies that reduce the cortisol surges through our sympathetic nervous system. Really, I want to emphasize the generativity that admiration and affection engender, which requires proximity and a coming together though not necessarily a community dynamic at play; it's as much about outlying affinity, difference, unselfish attachments, as well as desiring connections. I chose not to use quotation marks to delineate texts in order to heighten the porousness of ideation.

A special thanks to Jamie Townsend for his close reading of "Hyper Essay: Do We Pay at the Window?" Thanks to Tim Roberts and Julie Carr of Counterpath for bringing this work to life.

These sequences have appeared in the following publications:
Superflux, www.dcpoetry.com/anthology/2, Kadar Koli, Sous Rature, The Tangent
"Subsistence Equipment" was published as a chapbook by Faux Press.
"Early Linoleum" was published as a chapbook by Furniture Press.
"Glossematics, Thus" was published as a chapbook by Least Weasel Press.
"Atlantis" was published as a broadside by Trace Peterson, pre-EOUGH days.
"Meaning Meets Illusion" was published as a broadside by Aaron Tieger.

BRENDA IIJIMA's involvements occur at the often unnamable conjunctions and mutations of poetry, choreography, research movement, animal studies, speculative non-fiction and forlorn histories. She is the author of five full-length collections of poetry and numerous chapbooks and artist's books. She is also the editor of the *eco language reader* (Nightboat Books and PP@YYL). She is the editor of Portable Press at Yo-Yo Labs, located in Brooklyn, NY (http://yoyolabs.com/). The press published its 50th book this year.